THE MANUAL: THE ULTIMATE RESOURCE FOR CHRISTIANS

The Manual gave me inspiration as I was reading it and I believe I have started to make peace with everything that I have gone through. I have begun to change my way of thinking that everything does happen for a reason and God will never leave me alone and can give me all of the love that I have been seeking all of my life.

—K (online counseling client)

When reading the counseling section, I found high–quality information addressing some of the most challenging issues people face on a daily basis. I particularly like what you wrote about forgiveness. It was easy to understand, what for me has been difficult to put into words. The Manual will be an excellent resource for counselors, lay and Christian alike.

—Cathy Heyman
MA, NCC, LPCi
Licensed Professional Counselor Intern

THE MANUAL
The Ultimate Resource for Christians

THE MANUAL

The Ultimate Resource for Christians

Reverend Dawn Sutton MSW, RSW

TATE PUBLISHING & *Enterprises*

Published by Tate Publishing & Enterprises, LLC
127 E. Trade Center Terrace | Mustang, Oklahoma 73064 USA
1.888.361.9473 | www.tatepublishing.com

Tate Publishing is committed to excellence in the publishing industry. The company reflects the philosophy established by the founders, based on Psalm 68:11,
"The Lord gave the word and great was the company of those who published it."

Book design copyright © 2008 by Tate Publishing, LLC. All rights reserved.
Cover design by Stefanie Rooney
Interior design by Lindsay B. Behrens

Published in the United States of America

ISBN: 978-1-60604-478-0
1. Christian Living: Spiritual Growth: Completive Life
08.10.21

DEDICATION

This book is dedicated to all my clients who have had the courage to persevere despite their circumstances, who have continued to seek God's will in difficult times, and who have kept trusting in their Heavenly Father who attends them on their earthly journey and beyond. God bless you—and He will.

ACKNOWLEDGMENTS

I would like to acknowledge the two greatest blessings in my life: my sons, Dan and Josh. Thanks to Dan for his talent in graphic design for graphics work he has done on my counseling website. Thanks to Josh for all his work on designing and maintaining my website and general computer expertise. Most of all for their support.

Appreciation to my sister, Donna, for her help on my website. (Web Design—ladygnome@hotmail.com)

Thanks to David Douthitt (www.davestuff.us) for his fine web design ministry, upgrading my Web site (www.sunrisecounselling.com).

I would also like to thank pastors Stephen Brown, Bill Coleman, Gord Naismith, Sharon Wilson, and Al Smith for their support and encouragement.

Appreciation to Terry Mosley (www.morning–star.com) for her prayer support.

Thanks to my friends: Kathryn and Rodney, Betty, Richard, Adrienne, Pam, Marie, and Eve.

Most of all, I have to thank my God and Heavenly Father who made this book and everything else in my life possible.

TABLE OF CONTENTS

FOREWORD

In this day and age, it is not easy living a life in the spirit, but then again I don't believe it was in Lot's day either! As Christians, some obstacles are in clear view and scream, "Danger, danger!" and yet there are other obstacles in our walk that seem to be grey areas.

Surely, God didn't say I couldn't have this or do that? That age old snake is still trying to fool some of us! We need to know God personally and allow *Him* to change our character and lifestyle. *"I have been crucified with Christ; it is no longer I who live, but Christ who lives in me; and the life which I now live in the flesh I live by faith in the Son of God, who loved me and gave Himself for me" (Galatians 2:20).*

I believe that we are corporate within the faith. That is why we are called a "body"—the body of believers. Dawn has at many times entered into that corporateness of accountability with myself; a submitting to one another so that we may not be deceived or tricked by the evil one. Together we can stand. *"One can put a thousand to flight, but when they co–labor together, two can put ten thousand to flight" (Leviticus 26:8).*

Corporateness in the Body of Christ *is* the shield of protection that we all need. Dawn writes out of her own experiences in her walk with the Lord. Hebrews 5:8 says, *"Although He was a Son, He learned obedience from the things which He suf-*

fered." A once broken woman and humble in spirit, I believe Dawn has imparted her wisdom throughout the pages of The Manual *in describing what it means to be kept on the highway to holiness—a passionate journey.*

—Rev. Sharon Willson MCC BTh CCSW
Ezekiel Ministries

INTRODUCTION

If you are reading this and you are a new Christian, let me take this opportunity to warmly welcome you to the family of God. This book will provide you with information about biblical principles, spiritual lessons, and how to grow in your faith that would normally take many, many years!

You might want to think of it as "Bible Boot Camp Training." If you think of soldiers in an army, they always have to go through basic training before they are sent out to meet the enemy. The training is vigorous and thorough but when they have completed basic training, they should know everything they need to know in order to handle numerous situations in enemy lands.

We, as Christians, need to be prepared as well—spiritually. Often, new Christians experience wonderful answers to prayer and many blessings. After they have been Christians for a number of years, however, and if they really want to please and serve God, invariably they seem to go through many trials and tribulations and sometimes even horrific tragedies.

If they have been prepared by being built up in the truth, which is the Word of God, and if they have developed a good foundation of faith and prayer in their personal relationship with God, then they will be much better equipped to deal with adversity. It may come in different forms and in different areas of their lives, but it will come at some time.

So, as the carpenter needs the right tools to make beautiful pieces of furniture and as the soldier needs to understand strategy and have the right weapons to do as well as possible in warfare, so the Christian needs the right information to know how to live a victorious Christian life regardless of the circumstances one may face at any given time.

If you have been a Christian for some time, you have probably already discovered that the Christian life is not always an easy life. Most of us who have been Christians for a number of years know that there may be times when we need all the help we can get to deal with whatever has come our way.

Ideally, when we first give our hearts and lives to the Lord and accept Jesus as our personal Lord and Savior, we have spiritual mentors to disciple us. These are mature Christians and pastors who help us to get established in a local church, who teach us the Word of God, instruct us about biblical principles, and so forth.

The truth is that even those who have had such spiritual mentors may still find themselves struggling as Christians in different areas of their lives or in relation to their personal and spiritual growth. As a Christian counsellor for many years doing face–to–face counselling as well as internet counselling, I began to notice recurring themes in regards to problems and issues that Christians were facing. I also recognized that there were patterns with advice in response. This book is meant to address those issues that seem most prevalent to Christians.

There are any number of reasons why a person who has been a Christian for some period of time may find oneself feeling depressed, disillusioned, or discouraged. People who have had very traumatic childhoods, for example, have a host of issues to overcome from their past including inner healing, forgiveness, self–esteem, negative thinking patterns, and so on.

Others have difficulty with lifestyle choices and habitual sins that prevent them from living a successful Christian life. Others have dedicated themselves wholly to God and because of their fervor in attempting to serve Him, they face numerous adversities from the enemy as spiritual opposition that may simply wear them out over time.

Whatever you may be facing in your life right now, whether as a result of your past or due to present circumstances, I want you to know that there is help and there is hope and you can overcome any obstacles or tribulations in your life. At the end of each chapter, you will find appropriate Bible verses on that particular topic as well as resources for further assistance.

If you are reading this and you are not sure of your salvation or what it means to live a Christian life, perhaps you have never acknowledged that Jesus Christ died in your place for your sins.

Romans 3:22–26 (Good News Version) explains salvation this way:

> God puts people right through their faith in Jesus Christ. God does this to all who believe in Christ, because there is no difference at all: everyone has sinned and is far away from God's saving presence. But by the free gift of God's grace all are put right with Him through Christ Jesus, who sets them

free. God offered Him, so that by His sacrificial death He should become the means by which people's sins are forgiven through their faith in Him.

If you haven't already confessed your sins and accepted Jesus' sacrifice on the cross for each one of them, now is the time. It's as simple as saying something like: "Lord, I choose to believe that Jesus took my place on the cross for my sins and that He died and rose again on the third day. I am sorry for my sins. Please come into my heart and my life. Help me to surrender my life to you now, to live as you intended me to, and to bring you glory. Thank you for saving me, in Jesus' name, amen."

People experience salvation or being "born again" spiritually in different ways. Some have a specific spiritual experience or revelation that is glorious and unmistakable. Others quietly invite Jesus into their lives as their Saviour and nothing major happens at that exact moment, but over time, they develop a close, personal relationship with God and continue to grow in their faith.

I always feel a little odd sharing my salvation experience because it happened while I was watching TV! It was Easter time in the 70s and I was doing what I thought people did at Easter time: watching a religious movie. There was a really good mini-series on that year called "Jesus of Nazareth." At the very end of the movie, there was a close up of the actor playing Jesus and he said, "And, lo, I am with you always, even til the end of age" (Matthew 28:20).

At that moment, however, I was no longer watching TV because it was as if the real Jesus Christ Himself was speaking to me directly! It took me by surprise; I had not been praying for any revelation or anything at the time. I had always believed there was a God and that Jesus was His son, but I didn't know how to know Him personally. Suddenly, I had the distinct and very real understanding that Jesus really was real. And not just real, but alive and well!

Then my life flashed before me as described by people in perilous situations, except I wasn't about to die. Somehow I knew that I had committed many sins in my life that had offended God even though the word "sin" had never been a part of my vocabulary before.

I was practically overwhelmed with remorse, and on my knees, I wept profusely and asked God to forgive me. I suddenly comprehended that He was Holy and I was a sinner in His sight. Then, my entire being was flooded with a feeling of being loved that I had never known before and a sense of complete peace settled in my heart and spirit. Even so, I struggled for about six months with the decision to actually give God control over my life and make Him my Lord as well as my Saviour. Thankfully, it has never been the same since and I have never been the same since!

Whether you have just prayed that prayer for the first time or you have been a Christian for many years now, you will find valuable information and resources in each chapter to equip you emotionally and spiritually to deal with a variety of situations, problems, and dilemmas. God bless you as you grow deep in your faith, as you get established in His word, and learn how to live for His purposes and for His glory.

Part One:

BASIC TRAINING FOR CHRISTIANS

If any of you lacks wisdom, he should pray to God who will give it to him, because God gives generously and graciously to all. But when you pray, you must believe and not doubt at all.

James 1: 5–6 (Good News Version)

An acronym of the word BIBLE is *Basic Instruction Before Leaving Earth*. Knowing the Word of God is not only crucial for renewing your mind as a Christian, but it is a handbook on how to live our lives and how to please God. Whether you have just accepted Jesus Christ as your personal Saviour or whether you have years of service as a committed Christian, it is important to remember that Jesus invites us to keep learning and growing: "Come, all of you who are tired from carrying heavy loads, and I will give you rest. Take my yoke and put it on you, and learn from me."

(Matthew 11:28)

PRAYER

One can't say enough about prayer and that is why you can find a host of books on the subject discussing various aspects of prayer. It is the crux of our relationship with God. Believe that God answers your prayers because He does—perhaps not always "yes" or immediately, but He hears every prayer and answers each one. Thank God that He doesn't always give us what we want. He knows better than us what we really need and we have to trust Him about that.

People will inevitably be disappointed if they expect a Santa Clause type of response from God. Remember, as someone once said, He is our shield and buckler, not our chef and butler! Psalm 37:4 is a favorite verse of many, "Delight thyself also in the Lord; and He shall give thee the desires of thine heart." I don't personally believe, however, that verse means that if you love and acknowledge the Lord in your life, He will give you whatever you desire. I think it specifically refers to the prayers that you pray that involve loving Him more, serving Him better, growing spiritually, being more loving—any prayers that will glorify Him.

Prayer involves requests, praise and worship, thanking Him, seeking His will, and waiting on Him to speak to our hearts and minds. Most of all, it is our way of communing with God on a personal level and spending time with Him to draw closer to Him and to know Him better. That is the reason He created us after all, to have fellowship with us.

Some people have a set time for these devotions every day; however, many people (including myself) prefer an open, running dialogue with the Lord that continues throughout the day or evening regardless of wherever they may be: first thing in the morning, last thing at night, in the car driving, at home, at work, in a store, wherever and whenever. Prayer is a way of practicing God's presence; every time you speak to Him, you remind yourself that He is with you, that He cares about all the little things that occur in your everyday life no matter how trivial, and that He is not only our help but our companion and our friend.

Jesus tells us how and what to pray in Matthew 6:5–15 where we find the Lord's Prayer. There is great power in united prayer: a mighty and necessary weapon for the Body of Christ (Matthew 18:20). Confession of the Word of God in prayer can be important as well. The "Prayers that Avail Much" volumes by Word Ministries, Inc. are wonderful for using scripture references for praying specific, powerful prayers.

READING AND KNOWING THE WORD OF GOD

I cannot stress how important it is for Christians to know the Word of God. It is absolutely essential if we are to know what God requires of us, if we are to reach spiritual maturity, and if we are to be able to discern truth from error (false doctrine). Second Timothy 2:15 admonishes us to really know the Bible, "Study to shew thyself approved unto God, a workman that needeth not to be ashamed, rightly dividing the word of truth."

Joshua 1:8 emphasizes the importance of this again, "Be sure that the book of the Law is always read in your worship. Study it day and night, and make sure that you obey everything written in it. Then you will be prosperous and successful." I tell my counselling clients to "become one with the Word"—that is to read it, breathe it, eat it, drink it, meditate on it, refer to it, confess it, and so forth until it is deep down inside of them and part of their automatic thinking process.

We have so much negative thinking from our past to overcome and the bible tells us in Romans 12:2 to renew our minds in this manner. We need to replace lies with truth, essentially with God's truth. If you don't like reading, then get DVDs or listen to the Word by audiotapes but it is crucial as a Christian that you know God's Word! Memorize as many verses as you possibly can, especially those that are particularly helpful for you personally.

How can I know that the Bible is true? In John 7:16–17, "Jesus answered, What I teach is not my own teaching, but it comes from God, who sent me. Whoever is willing to do what God wants will know whether what I teach comes from God or whether I speak on my own authority."

How can I understand the Bible? Luke 11:13, "How much more then will the Father in heaven give the Holy Spirit to those who ask Him!"

If you are a new Christian and having difficulty with the Old English of the King James Version check out the modern day English versions of the Bible such as "The Message" at your local Christian bookstore or online.

ATTENDING A PLACE OF WORSHIP

Unfortunately many people tell themselves that it is okay to be a follower of Christ and not attend church services. Hebrews 10:25 clearly states, however, "Let us not give up the habit of meeting together, as some are doing. Instead, let us encourage one another all the more, since you see that the Day of the Lord is drawing near."

Going to church regularly is very important for a number of reasons: mutual support and encouragement, to grow spiritually, to be used of God according to the abilities He has given you in the body of Christ, and for a sense of belonging in the family of God, to name a few.

Not all churches are alike, however, and it is important to find the one God wants you to attend. If you are having trouble finding a good church in your area, check out www.churchangel.com. There are many churches these days that have Web sites and even audio samples of sermons so that you can get a sense of whether that is a church God might want you to look into before even going there in person. A good church will focus on the Word of God and be evangelical and will not shy away from expounding on the hard truths of the Bible that help us grow and keep us in a right relationship with God.

If you are a Christian but have not been attending church because you are disappointed with church politics or because of a pastor or any other reason, please read Michael Fackerell's article "Christians out of Church."[1]

BAPTISM IN WATER

"Go ye therefore, and teach all nations, baptizing them in the name of the Father, and of the Son, and of the Holy Ghost" (Matthew 28:19). We are commanded to be baptized in water once we have accepted Jesus as our Saviour. It is a step of obedience in your Christian walk. Jesus publicly died on the cross for your sins and it should be considered a privilege to publicly declare your new faith in Him. When you go under the water (full immersion) it is like leaving behind the "old you" and leaving your sinful past behind and when you come up out of the water, it is like starting over as a new creation in Christ Jesus (2 Corinthians 5:17, Colossians 2:12).

If you haven't already been baptized in water but you are professing to be a Christian, you need to take this step as soon as possible. It will make a difference in your spiritual growth. Jesus Himself was baptized in water as our example (Matthew 3:13–16). "Peter said to them, Each one of you must turn away from his sins and be baptized in the name of Jesus Christ, so that your sins will be forgiven and you will receive God's gift, the Holy Spirit" (Acts 2:38). Read the account of the Ethiopian official who said to Philip, "Here is some water. What is to keep me from being baptized? The official was baptized, then and there—what, then, is preventing you from being baptized?" (Acts 8: 36–40).

THE TEN COMMANDMENTS

There are some straightforward commands in the Bible including the Ten Commandments, which are the primary *don'ts* (Exodus 20:3–17). Though self–explanatory, it is interesting that there is one command that has a condition attached to it, "Honor thy father and mother: that as the Lord thy God commanded thee; that thy days may be prolonged, and that it may go well with thee, in the land which the Lord thy God giveth thee" (Deuteronomy 5:16).

Some would say the implication here, then, is that if one does not honor their mother or father, that it may not go well with them. It is important not to judge your mother or father, even if they have not been good parents, and to forgive them for their weaknesses and mistakes. In fact, Matthew 15:4 says, "For God said, respect your father and your mother and whoever curses his father or his mother is to be put to death."

Craig Hill has an entire ministry based on biblical "Ancient Paths." It covers all the ways a mother or father can bless or curse their own children and then goes on to explain why it is so important to forgive and honor your parents. If you have had a lot of unresolved issues with your parents, it may be very helpful for you to attend one of the Ancient Path seminars.[2]

RESTITUTION

We are promised in 1 John 1: 9 that if we confess our sins, then we are forgiven; however, people who repent are required, if possible, to produce the fruit of repentance in their lives. (Matthew 3:8). After his conversion, Paul declared that he had been sent to different areas and then to the Gentiles so "that they should repent and turn to God, and do works meet for repentance" (Acts 26:20). Restitution is a demonstration of repentance, then, in accordance with the Word of God to satisfy the righteousness of God (Romans 13:7–10).

Restitution involves restoration to the offended party— whatever was lost through injury to reputation, life, limb, or property or which was destroyed, lost, stolen, or damaged due to one's sin, negligence or carelessness. Restitution was commanded in the Law initially (Exodus 21:26–36), was affirmed by John the Baptist (Luke 3:7–14), and practiced by Zacchaeus the chief tax collector (Luke 19:8, 9). Jesus directed His followers to settle any claims that anyone had against them even before going to the Lord in worship (Matthew 5:23, 24).

I know of people who stole money or items or shoplifted and then became Christians. They made restitution by paying back the value of whatever they stole. They put a letter in with the funds explaining that they had accepted Jesus as their Saviour and that act of restitution in itself became an opportunity to witness to others. Of course, it isn't always possible to make restitution, if you stole from a company that is no longer in business, for example, or if you are unable to track down a certain individual. If there is any way you can make restitution or restore a relationship, however, make every effort to right the wrong.

EVANGELISM

The Bible speaks of "The Great Commission:" to win souls to Christ by spreading the gospel. "And he said unto them, Go ye into all the world, and preach the gospel to every creature" (Mark 15:15). God does not wish anyone to go to hell (2 Peter 2:9) and obviously we should share in His burden to bring others to a saving knowledge of Jesus Christ.

Not everyone has an anointed gifting or a specific calling to be an evangelist, but we all know people who are not saved and God can use you to witness to others. Of course, it is important that you are a living witness as well, that your life, behaviors, and your attitudes are in line with the Word of God. If you witness to others, it should be out of concern for their eternal welfare and not in any judgmental way.

There seems to be an even greater urgency these days because many believe that the time is short and Jesus will return soon. We all need to be prepared to share our faith with others as much as possible. Daniel 12:3 declares, "And they that be wise shall shine as the brightness of the firmament; they that turn many to righteousness as the stars for ever and ever." If you don't have a burden for lost souls, pray for this. Revelation 14:15 states, "For the time is come for thee to reap; for the harvest of the earth is ripe."

There is an article by Rev. Leslie McSpadden[3] that explains six styles of evangelism: confrontational, intellectual, testimonial, relational, invitational, and service. See which style describes your personal style.

In all our lives, in all the things we will ever do and accomplish, the highest thing we can do is lead another person to the saving knowledge of Christ and/or to help them grow in their faith and righteousness.

TO LOVE YOUR NEIGHBOR AS YOURSELF

This is the command in Galatians 5:14, "For the whole law is summed up in one commandment: Love your neighbor as you love yourself." The assumption here, however, is that you already love yourself, not in any conceited, boastful way, of course, but in a healthy, positive way. The Bible reminds us that our body is the temple of the Holy Spirit so we are to take care of ourselves physically so that we are in good health. It is also important to nurture ourselves and be kind to ourselves, to treat ourselves as we would treat a best friend. It is when we truly love and accept ourselves that we can love others well and are able to receive their love for us. First Corinthians 13:1–3 says it well,

"I may be able to speak the languages of man and even of angels, but if I have no love, my speech is no more than a noisy gong or clanging bell. I may have the gift of inspired, preaching: I may have all knowledge and understand all secrets; I may have all the faith needed to move mountains—but if I have no love, I am nothing. I may give away everything I have, and even give up my body to be burned but if I have no love, this does me no good."

TO LOVE GOD WITH EVERYTHING YOU HAVE AND ARE

In Matthew 22:37, "Jesus said unto him, Thou shalt love the Lord thy God with all thy heart, and with all thy soul, and with all thy mind." This means always acknowledging God and seeking His will for your life. It means putting Him first in your life. It means trying on a daily basis to do His will and to become the person He wants you to be. It means being obedient. It means spending time with Him and communing with Him and desiring to be even closer to Him. It means self–denial. It means choosing to trust Him when your circumstances are very difficult and painful. It means choosing to believe He loves you when you don't feel His love or His presence or it doesn't look like He is hearing or answering your prayers. It means never giving up your faith in Him.

TITHING

How to Heal Your Finances—Tithe!

Hal Weeks[4] has written this wonderful article on tithing. First, whether tithing is required of a Christian or whether it was only binding under the Old Covenant is an issue for many Christians.

> "I the Lord do not change. So you, O descendants of Jacob, are not destroyed. Ever since the time of your forefathers you have turned away from my decrees and have not kept them. Return to me, and I will return to you," says the Lord Almighty. "But you ask, 'How are we to return? Will a man rob God?' Yet you rob me. But you ask, 'How do we rob you?' In tithes and offerings. You are under a curse—the whole nation of you—because you are robbing me. Bring the whole tithe into the storehouse, that there may be food in my house. Test me in this," says the Lord Almighty, "and see if I will not throw open the floodgates of heaven and pour out so much blessing that you will not have room enough for it. I will prevent pests from devouring your crops, and the vines in your fields will not cast their fruit," says the LORD Almighty. "Then all the nations will call you blessed, for yours will be a delightful land," says the Lord Almighty. Malachi 3:6–12 (NIV)

Here we discover tithing was indeed required of the Israelites under the Old Covenant. Here God is challenging those who tithe to see if He will not bless them beyond their capacity to receive it. Most theologians believe that tithing is relevant to today as well. If you are having financial struggles, I challenge you to start tithing. There are many testimonies by those who have found this solved their financial problems. Is the tithe to be before or after taxes? Some believe that it should be a tenth of our total income because our taxes are just part of our expenses, like food and clothing.

You may also give offerings over and above the 10% tithe to Christian organizations or any charity God lays on your heart. I believe you can tithe in other ways as well, such as when you use your talents and your time for the Lord. Are you also tithing 10% of your time to the Lord?

COMMUNION

We are encouraged to participate in communion to remember our Lord and Jesus' sacrifice for us upon the Cross. It is also provides the opportunity to examine ourselves to see if we have any recent unconfessed sin in our lives or any attitudes toward God and/or others that are not pleasing to Him. There is a warning, however, so it is important that you do not take communion if you are not born again spiritually or without examining yourself first.

> This means that every time you eat this bread and drink from this cup you proclaim the Lord's death until he comes. It follows that if anyone eats the Lord's bread or drinks from his cup in a way that dishonors him he is guilty of sin against the Lord's body and blood. So, then everyone should examine himself first, and then eat the bread and drink from the cup. For if he does not recognize the meaning of the Lord's body when he eats the bread and drinks from the cup, he brings judgment on himself as he eats and drinks. That is why many of you are sick and weak, and several have died.
>
> 1 Corinthians 11:26–30

THE GIFTS OF THE HOLY SPIRIT

All gifts of the Holy Spirit are meant to unite and build up the body of Christ. It is up to God to give "to each one individually as He wills" (1 Corinthians 12:11). The verses that highlight the gifts of the Holy Spirit are:

> To one is given through the Spirit the message of wisdom, to another the message of knowledge by means of the same spirit, to another faith by the same Spirit, to another gifts of healing by that one Spirit, to another miraculous powers, to another prophecy, to another distinguishing between spirits, to another speaking in different kinds of tongues, and to still another, the interpretation of tongues.
>
> 1 Corinthians 12:8–11 (NIV)

> It was he who gave some to be apostles, some to be prophets, some to be evangelists, and some to be pastors and teachers, to prepare God's people for works of service so that the body of Christ may be built up.
>
> Ephesians 4:11–12 (NIV)

1 Corinthians 12:31 encourages us to "earnestly desire" the gifts of the Holy Spirit and we are accountable for the use of any gifts that God chooses to bless us with. "As each one has received a gift, minister it to one another, as good stewards of the manifold grace of God" (1 Peter 4:10).

There is a spiritual inventory to assess your spiritual gifts in the chapter "Priorities/Your Purpose in Life."

HEALING

God heals us in many ways. There is healing through confession of sin, healing of emotional wounds through God's love, healing of memories, healing through forgiveness, and healing of physical ailments.

Jesus healed people of any number of diseases (Matthew 4:23), and gifts of healing are given to believers to minister to those in need (1 Corinthians 12:8–11). We are also exhorted in James 5:13–16 "to bring those who are sick for prayer."

I have personally experienced healing several times as a Christian. I was diagnosed with Irritable Bowel Syndrome and the doctors told me I would have it the rest of my life. I decided to stand on the Word of God and claim my healing: 1 Peter 2:24, "By whose stripes ye were healed." I kept on confessing that the Lord would heal me, even though I suffered with pain on a daily basis. Of course, God chooses to heal us in His way and in His time. Often it is through doctors and medicine or with surgery. I found a herbal remedy that helped me manage the pain temporarily, but I still wanted complete healing.

After a year and a half of taking the herbal remedy several times a day, I attended a healing service (led by an evangelical Catholic priest) and I went up for prayer. I was "slain in the Spirit" (fell down under the power of God) and as I lay on the floor, I felt God do a work in me. After that I was healed!

Another time I had symptoms of a kidney infection and was in a lot of pain. A friend of mine, Karen, put her hand on my shoulder and prayed for me in her home. I felt something warm go down through my body and my symptoms disappeared. These are only two examples of physical healing in one Christian life. I knew a young man who had cancer in the lymph nodes and he was healed by God. There are countless accounts of healings experienced by Christians today.

What of those who don't get healed? I am thinking here of Paul who prayed for relief of an affliction and did not receive it. "And he said unto me, My grace is sufficient for thee: for my strength is made perfect in weakness. Most gladly therefore will I rather glory in my infirmities, that the power of Christ may rest upon me" (2 Corinthians 12:8–10).

God always answer prayer; He may choose to heal you spiritually or emotionally if He feels that will benefit you more than physical healing at the time. Or He may choose to heal you when you have moved on to your life in Heaven. We can trust and believe that God is a good and loving God and if you are not healed right away or in the way you expect, then He has a good and loving reason, which is somehow in your best interest for the time being. It makes me think of Joni Eareckson Tada. [5]God didn't choose to heal her physically from paralysis but He has used her in phenomenal ways through her art, her testimony, and her books for His glory and to minister to others. Trust in His higher wisdom (Isaiah 55:8).

THE FRUIT OF THE SPIRIT

The fruits of the Spirit are listed in Galatians 5:22–23: "Love, joy, peace, patience, kindness, goodness, faithfulness, gentleness and self–control" (NIV). They can be used as a spiritual yardstick to assess our maturity as Christians. How do we achieve this kind of maturity? We need to surrender ourselves to the Holy Spirit. Remember we are to "love the Lord thy God with all thy heart, and with all thy soul, and with all thy mind" (Matthew 22:37).

Are you dead to sin? Sin should no longer have control over you. Paul said, "I have been crucified with Christ; it is no longer I who live, but Christ lives in me" (Romans 6:12–13). Are you surrendered to Him? Mind, body, will, soul? Of course, this doesn't mean that God expects us to demonstrate all the fruit of the Spirit overnight. We might have to work on one attribute at a time and it is something you will continue to work on throughout your life.

BIGGER QUESTIONS

If you are still struggling with questions about the Christian faith such as: proving the validity of the Bible, explaining the Trinity, the credibility of miracles, whether other religions are compatible with Christianity, the fate of those who haven't heard the gospel, if the Bible allows for the theory of evolution, etc. then I would recommend the book *Answers to Tough Questions* by Josh McDowell or the Web site http://www.rbc.org/questions/Answers to tough questions.

BAPTISM OF THE HOLY SPIRIT

I do not wish to spark any theological debates here. I will cite verses that I believe acknowledge the baptism of the Holy Spirit for the present times. I can also say, however, that no matter who you are or what denomination you adhere to or no matter what your theological training, you cannot argue with someone's personal experience. I have received the baptism of the Holy Spirit and I can speak in tongues and I know countless others that have had the same experience, which has powerfully transformed their spiritual understanding and growth.

This is how I see the difference of having and not having it if we liken it to computers. You can have a computer that offers the basic functions, such as some word processing programs and which would allow you to perform basic activities. If, however, you connect to the Internet, it is like an entirely new world that you can then access. There is a quite a difference!

As Christians, we can function without the baptism of the Holy Spirit, but we are capable of so much more if we have the baptism of the Holy Spirit. This means more joy, more peace, more love, a better understanding of the Word, more revelation, a closer walk with God, being a better witness, etc. It's a free gift and the Bible says to ask for it. You need to be hungry for God, to want to be closer to Him, to know Him better, to be a better Christian—but what a difference it makes to live a victorious Christian life. It's that extra power to overcome sin and evil in our lives as well.

I will never forget when it happened to me. I had been a Christian for about two and a half years, but I was eager to be even closer to God, to know His will for my life, to serve Him in any way possible, and so forth. At that point, however, I didn't really know much about the baptism of the Holy Spirit. I attended a conference in Toronto, Canada by Jim and Tammy Bakker (years ago before the scandal). Before they spoke, the worship team was leading the audience and we were singing the "Hallelujah Chorus." Everyone was holding hands raised in the air.

Suddenly, it was like a surge of electricity running through those connected hands going through one person into the next and so on. When this electrical–like current approached me, I had a tremendous spiritual experience! Even though I was well aware that my feet were planted solidly on the floor, it was as though I was about fifteen feet above the floor. It is really hard to describe but it was as though my spirit was somewhere else and, suddenly, somehow, I knew that I was standing in the presence of God Himself!

I didn't see God; I just knew I was before Him somehow and I was totally blown away by the sense of His power and majesty I was experiencing. Later, I tried to describe God's greatness and there were no English words that would come close to describing how amazing, how awesome, how powerful God is. I think the closest description I could come up with was "almighty" but that concept then magnified many, many times over.

I continued with the worship but I was changed forever. I couldn't wipe the smile off my face for two weeks! I had a boldness I didn't have before to share my faith with others. I felt full of joy and peace and experienced a sense of complete well–being. When I read the Bible, it was like reading a brand new book that I never read previously because I could understand so much more than I did before. I didn't know about speaking in tongues at that point. I was puzzled about that once I learned about the baptism of the Holy Spirit because I had understood that speaking in tongues was part of the experience and the evidence of the baptism of the Holy Spirit.

I was absolutely convinced, however, that I had indeed received the baptism of the Holy Spirit because it was a life–changing experience and revolutionized my spiritual growth. About a year later, I was in my bedroom praying before going to bed when suddenly, this feeling bubbled up inside of me, and out of nowhere, out came this foreign language with no effort on my part whatsoever!

I have been speaking in an unknown tongue for about twenty–eight years now and once at a church service out of town, I was standing behind a woman during worship and she used the same words, the same language, whatever it is! So, I know it's real and that when I pray in tongues, it is "spirit to spirit" since God is a spirit and that He knows what I am saying. "The one who speaks in tongues does not speak to others but to God, because no one understands him. He is speaking secret truths by the power of the Spirit" (1 Corinthians 14:2).

The Baptism in the Holy Spirit
and How to Receive It [6]

Hal Weeks has written the following article on the baptism of the Holy Spirit.

As always, we must first define our terms so what is said is clearly understood. The word "baptism" is from the Greek word "baptize," which means to immerse.[7] Therefore, the baptism in the Holy Spirit means to be immersed in the Holy Spirit. This immersion is distinct from being baptized in water as the sign of conversion. It is usually a subsequent event. Scripture uses other expressions that also refer to this experience. They are "being filled with the Holy Spirit," "receiving the gift of the Holy Spirit," "the Holy Spirit coming upon them," and, "the Holy Spirit being poured out upon them." Scripture also uses some of these expressions to refer to other works of the Holy Spirit.

Baptism in the Holy Spirit always refers to what happened to the disciples at Pentecost. Since the word "baptize" comes from a Greek word that means to immerse, the use of the preposition "in" is consistent with that understanding. We are immersed *in* the Holy Spirit, not immersed by the Holy Spirit or immersed with the Holy Spirit.

What is the Difference Between Being Baptized in Water and Being Baptized in the Holy Spirit?

Specifically, there are three baptisms mentioned in Scripture that apply to the believer:

1. Being baptized into the body of Christ (Christ being the element by the Holy Spirit [the Holy Spirit being the

agent). "For we were all baptized by one Spirit into one body—whether Jews or Greeks, slave or free—and we were all given the one Spirit to drink" (1 Corinthians 12:13, NIV).

2. Being baptized in water (water being the element) by the minister (the minister being the agent).

3. Being baptized in the Holy Spirit (the Holy Spirit being the element): "I (John the Baptist) indeed baptize you with water to repentance: but he that comes after me (Jesus Christ) is mightier than I, whose shoes I am not worthy to bear: he shall baptize you in the Holy Ghost, and with fire" (Matthew 3:11). Being baptized in water is done by a clergy person. The candidate is baptized (immersed) in the element of water. This usually occurs shortly after conversion. Being baptized in the Holy Spirit can occur at any time after being born again.

So what is the difference between being baptized in water and being baptized in the Holy Spirit?

In the first case, we are filled with the Holy Spirit. We become a "well of living water." In the second case, we are filled to overflowing, and become "rivers of living water." These rivers of living water generate the power and boldness we need to carry out God's purpose for us. "But whosoever drinks of the water that I shall give him shall never thirst; but the water that I shall give him shall be in him a well of (living) water springing up into everlasting life" (John 4:14).

> In the last day, that great day of the feast, Jesus stood and cried, saying, If any man thirst, let him come to me, and drink. He that believes on me, as the Scripture has said, out

of his innermost being shall flow rivers of living water. (But this spoke he of the Spirit, which they that believe on him should receive: for the Holy Spirit was not yet given; because Jesus was not yet glorified" (ascended to Heaven).

John 7:37–39

Why do we need the baptism of the Holy Spirit? Christ is our example. Before Jesus himself could begin His earthly ministry, He had to be baptized in the Holy Spirit. Before the disciples could begin their ministry, they had to be baptized in the Holy Spirit. This is what happened on the day of Pentecost. Should we then think it strange that we also need this baptism for ministry? In reality, Scripture says we will be called upon to do even greater works than Jesus (John 14:12).

Can't we witness to others without the baptism of the Holy Spirit? Yes, and there are many in ministry who do not profess to having been baptized in the Holy Spirit. Some even teach against it. Also, there are some who privately profess to being baptized in the Holy Spirit and speaking in tongues but have never publicly acknowledged it. Nevertheless, it is God's provision for equipping us to carry out what He commissions us to do. Christ commanded His disciples to remain in Jerusalem until they had received this. Scripture confirms that they were much more effective after their experience on Pentecost than they were before. Also, there are a multitude of Christians today who acknowledge they were unable to witness, at least effectively, until they had been baptized in the Holy Spirit.

And, being assembled together with them, commanded them that they should not depart from Jerusalem, but wait for the promise of the Father, which, says he, you have heard of me. For John truly baptized with water; but you shall be baptized with the Holy Spirit not many days hence…But you shall receive power, after that the Holy Spirit is come upon you: and you shall be witnesses to me both in Jerusalem, and in all Judea, and in Samaria, and to the uttermost part of the earth.

(Acts 1: 4–6,8)

Do you need to speak in tongues? It is not a question of do you need to, but do you get to! The basic question is, "Do you trust God?" Speaking in tongues is the scriptural objective evidence of having received this power. By definition, evidence means that it is something that can be seen and heard by others. The subjective evidence which we can't see are many. These can be personally overwhelming, though they may or may not be noticeable to others.

What good does it do to speak in a language we do not understand? First, this becomes available to us when we receive the baptism in the Holy Spirit, and the Holy Spirit wants us to have it! If we trust Him that should be reason enough. However, because God can only reach the heart of most of us by way of our intellect, the following is offered: tongues is also called a prayer language. Since this prayer language is given to us by the Holy Spirit, it makes it possible to pray perfectly. Because we don't know what we are praying, our intellect is bypassed. So this kind of prayer is never hindered by our ignorance, doubts, fears, unbelief, and human reasoning.

There are times when, as the Scripture says, we do not know how to pray. Praying in the spirit (tongues) solves this problem." (1 Cor. 4:2) We are in spiritual warfare. The devil cannot decipher praying in tongues. Thus, we can pray to God in a secret code. (Romans 8:26–27) Praying in the spirit (tongues) edifies us (build or charges us up spiritually). (Eph. 6:16–18) "He who speaks in a tongue edifies himself, but he who prophesies edifies the church." (1 Corinthians 14:4)

How Do I Know Tongues Are Not From the Devil?

Not so much anymore, but some still teach that speaking in tongues is from the devil. The answer is simple! If we go to the right place, we get the right thing. If we go to a bank, we will not get counterfeit money. If we go to Jesus, we will receive the genuine; we will not receive the counterfeit.

> And I say to you, Ask, and it shall be given you; seek, and you shall find; knock, and it shall be opened to you. For everyone that asks receives; and he that seeks finds; and to him that knocks it shall be opened. If a son shall ask bread of any of you that is a father, will he give him a stone? Or if he asks a fish, will he for a fish give him a serpent? Or if he shall ask an egg, will he offer him a scorpion? If you then, being evil, know how to give good gifts to your children: how much more shall your heavenly Father give the Holy Spirit to them that ask him?
>
> (Luke 11:9–13)

That this "giving of the Holy Spirit" refers to the baptism in the Holy Spirit and not conversion is confirmed, because God refers to Himself as our Heavenly Father. This baptism in the Holy Spirit is only available to God's children.

What are some subjective evidences of the baptism of the Holy Spirit? A common discovery is that, since the Author now dwells in them, the Bible suddenly comes alive to them. They understand it in a way they never did before. They find themselves with a new boldness to tell others what Jesus Christ means to them. They see and experience, more and more, the manifestation of the spiritual gifts. They not only have a new boldness to witness, but they have a lot more to witness about! In time, and as they mature, they start bearing the fruits of the spirit.

How do I receive the baptism of the Holy Spirit? First, we must be born again and believe what the Scriptures say about it. This is an absolute prerequisite. Then the baptism in the Holy Spirit becomes available. The Scriptures give us the basic approach, but we must experience it personally. That is, be thirsty, go to Jesus, who is the Baptizer, and drink.

> In the last day, that great day of the feast, Jesus stood and cried, saying, If any man thirst, let him come to me, and drink. He that believes on me, as the Scripture has said, out of his belly shall flow rivers of living water. But this spoke he of the Spirit, which they that believe on him should receive: for the Holy Ghost was not yet given; because that Jesus was not yet glorified.
>
> (John 7:37–39)

Are there any hindrances to receiving this gift? Yes. Fear, pride, lack of trust in God, reluctance to surrender control of everything to the Holy Spirit, not being willing to risk embarrassment, holding unforgiveness, and holding unconfessed sin in our lives are all hindrances. If you have difficulty receiving, remember God wants you to have it. If you ask Him, the Holy Spirit will reveal anything that is hindering you, provided you are honest and receptive. Some have said, "If God wants me to have it, He will give it to me." True, He does want you to have it, but you must thirst for it, go to Jesus to get it, and drink it in. Remember, you did not receive your salvation with that approach.

Specifically, what do I do? Different groups have some individuality in the methods they employ for receiving the baptism in the Holy Spirit. For some, listening to two teaching tapes, "How to Receive the Holy Spirit," and, "How to Exercise Vocal Gifts" by Derek Prince, has been successful. Praying, with the "laying on of hands," is a common way, and is Scriptural. This is especially true when done by someone who has the baptism in the Holy Spirit.

Although, it is possible to receive the baptism in the Holy Spirit without the manifestation of speaking in tongues initially, it is a gift from Jesus who wants you to have it. All languages are made up of a series of syllables. Tongues is also made up of a series of syllables. The syllables will come to your mind as thoughts but will require you to utter them. You may receive this prayer language spontaneously or it may require some practice, like learning to whistle. In any case, God wants you to have it and the devil doesn't. Don't let the enemy deceive you into believing it is not for you. There is no scriptural basis why everyone can't receive it. Although there is no reason you can't receive it on your own, it may be useful to have a spirit–filled person pray for you.

> When the apostles in Jerusalem heard that Samaria had accepted the word of God, they sent Peter and John to them. When they arrived, they prayed for them that they might receive the Holy Spirit, because the Holy Spirit had not yet come upon any of them; they had simply been baptized into the name of the Lord Jesus. Then Peter and John placed their hands on them, and they received (the baptism in) the Holy Spirit. When Simon saw that the Spirit was given at the laying on of the apostles' hands, he offered them money and said, "Give me also this ability so that everyone on whom I lay my hands may receive the Holy Spirit."
>
> (Acts 8:14–19)

> While Apollos was at Corinth, Paul took the road through the interior and arrived at Ephesus. There he found some disciples and asked them, "Did you receive the Holy Spirit when you believed?" They answered, "No, we have not even heard that there is a Holy Spirit." So Paul asked, "Then what baptism did you receive?" "John's baptism," they replied. Paul said, "John's baptism was a baptism of repentance. He told the people to believe in the one coming after him, that is, in Jesus." On hearing this, they were baptized into the name of the Lord Jesus. When Paul placed his hands on them, the Holy Spirit came on them, and they spoke in tongues and prophesied.
>
> (Acts 19:1–6)

What if nothing seems to happen? Scripture says that when we receive it, we receive it by faith. That is, by trusting God. Experience teaches us there may be a need to persist until we receive it. Again, possibly there may be some hindrances we must deal with first. But, if we are diligent, we will receive it. It seems, also, that those who persevere in the face of apparent initial failure, receive a greater measure when they do receive.

Suggested Prayer for Receiving
the Baptism of the Holy Spirit

Note: Before saying this prayer, be sure you have accepted Jesus as your Lord and Savior.

"Dear Lord Jesus, I am thirsty. I want to go your way and do your thing. I come to you as the baptizer in the Holy Spirit. In obedience to your Word, I ask You to empower me to do my part in carrying out the Great Commission. I believe you provide us with all that you require of us if we will open ourselves to all that you have for us and simply receive. Therefore, I, by an act of my will and in obedience to your word, present myself as a living sacrifice, wholly and acceptable to you, which is my reasonable service. I ask you, Lord Jesus, to baptize me in the Holy Spirit with the evidence of speaking in other tongues as the Holy Spirit gives me the utterance. I receive it by faith. That is by a complete and total trust in you. Amen."

You can be sure the devil does not want you to have such a powerful weapon that you can use against him. He will put the thought in your mind that you are doing this. He will accuse you of doing it yourselves. Your reply is, "Yes, devil, I am doing the speaking myself, but it is the Holy Spirit who is giving me the words!" It may help to think of a language as a series of syllables and what will come into your thoughts will therefore be syllables. You may wonder if they are genuine but practice uttering them. With practice this often leads to getting the real thing.

Note: It is often helpful for someone to pray with you for the baptism in the Holy Spirit, someone or others who have already received the baptism of the Holy Spirit themselves.

Resources:

A Handbook on Holy Spirit Baptism by Don Basham

If you have read all of Part One and you have applied each concept to your Christian walk personally, then congratulations! You have completed Basic Training. Now, on to growing spiritually and maturing as a Christian.

Part Two:

DEVELOPING SPIRITUAL MATURITY

I have fed you with milk, and not with meat: for hitherto ye were not able to bear it, neither yet now are ye able.

(1 Corinthians 3:2)

PRAISE

The Bible says that if we don't praise God, the rocks and hills will praise Him. We are to praise and worship God simply because of who He is, regardless of any of our earthly circumstances.

Who is to praise Him?

Praise Him, hills and mountains, fruit trees and forests; all animals, tame and wild, reptiles and birds. Praise Him, kings and all peoples, princes and all other rulers; girls and young men, old people and children too. Let them all praise the name of the Lord.

Psalm 148:9–13

Why should we praise God?

It is pleasant and right to praise Him.

Psalm 147:2

What are we to praise Him for?

In every thing give thanks: for this is the will of God in Christ Jesus concerning you.

1 Thessalonians 5:18

Praise Him for the mighty things He has done.

Psalm 150:2

Praise His supreme greatness.

Psalm 150:2

Give thanks to the Lord because He is good; His love is eternal.

Psalm 136:1

Giving thanks is the sacrifice that honors me, and I will surely save all those who obey me.

Psalm 50:23

(There are far too many to list here.)

Where are we to praise Him?

Praise Him in the assembly of His faithful people.

Psalm 149:1

Praise God in his temple.

Psalm 150:1

How should we praise Him?

It is good to sing praise to our God.

Psalm 147:1

Let them shout aloud as they praise God.

Psalm 149:6

Praise Him with trumpets. Praise Him with harps and lyres. Praise Him with drums and dancing. Praise Him with flutes, cymbals....

Psalm 150:3–5

Raise your hands in prayer in the temple, and praise the Lord.

Psalm 134:2

I will praise you, Lord, with all my heart.

Psalm 9:1

Praise the Lord, my soul! All my being, praise His holy name.

Psalm 103:1

Worship the Lord with joy.

Psalm 100:2

Clap your hands for joy.

Psalm 47:1

When should we praise Him?

I will praise Him as long as I live.

Psalm 146:2

I will always praise the Lord.

Psalm 145:21

Seven times each day I thank you for your righteous judgments.

Psalm 119:164

I will never stop praising Him.

Psalm 34:1

Worship Him continually.

I Chronicles 16:11

The Bible's remedy for depression: "the garment of praise for the spirit of heaviness" (Isaiah 6:13) If we worship Him, especially in the midst of painful situations, God will often turn the situation around completely and bring something wonderful out of it.

A book that revolutionized my walk with the Lord was *Prison to Praise* by Chaplain Merlin R. Carothers. He cites examples of people praising God and thanking Him in the worst predicaments, and then they were blessed with the most amazing outcomes!

I can think of an example in my own life where it was necessary for me to work at a place where I did not want to work for several months. It was not simply a matter of not liking the work; it was actually detrimental to my health and well-being physically and emotionally. It was so bad that I would find myself crying on the way to work, asking God why I had to work there. As it turned out, some incredible blessings came out of that experience. From that trial, amongst others, I learned that we really can trust God, that He is working out something for our good even when a situation seems unbearable and we can make no sense of it all.

We need to develop an "attitude of gratitude." Try keeping a gratitude journal. Write down at least three things every day that you can thank God for. These can be anything from a good cup of coffee to a sunny day to appreciating your sight or vision to a warm bed or safe shelter, whatever. Make this a habit and every night before you go to bed, thank God for as many things as you can think of for that day. The moment you awaken, start praising God for a new day (Lamentations 3:22–23) for more opportunities to serve Him, for His goodness, His word, His faithfulness, His forgiveness, etc. Part of your daily devotions and prayer time should always include thanking God and praising Him. Make praising God a habit, whether you "feel" like doing it or not.

Hopefully, everyone reading this already knows that, as Christians, our priorities should be as follows: God, family/relationships, job, hobbies, etc. The keys are knowing your priorities and maintaining a balance in your life. It is imperative, especially for pastors and those in ministry, to ensure that they spend enough time with their family and that they have time for their own personal relationship with God. Your life is His gift to you; what you do with your life is your gift back to Him.

20 Things God Won't Ask
You on Judgment Day[8]

1. God won't ask you what kind of car you drove, but will ask how many people you drove who didn't have transportation.

2. God won't ask you about the square footage of your house, but will ask how many people you welcomed into your home.

3. God won't ask how much overtime you worked, but will ask if you worked overtime for those you love and more importantly those you do not.

4. God won't ask about the fancy clothes you had in your closet, but will ask how many others you helped clothe.

5. God won't ask about your social status, but will ask what kind of class you displayed.

6. God won't ask how many material possessions you had, but will ask if they dictated your life.

7. God won't ask how much money you made, but will ask how much you selfishly kept for yourself.

8. God won't ask what your high salary was, but will ask if you compromised your character to obtain that salary.

9. God won't ask how many promotions you received, but will ask how you promoted others.

10. God won't ask what your job title was, but will ask if you performed your job to the best of your ability.

11. God won't ask what you did to help yourself, but will ask what you did to help others.

12. God won't ask how many friends you had, but will ask how many people to whom you were a friend.

13. God won't ask what you did to protect your rights, but will ask what you did to protect the rights of others.

14. God won't ask in what neighborhood you lived, but will ask you how you treated your neighbours.

15. God won't ask about what you did just on Sunday, but will ask what you did Monday through Saturday.

16. God won't ask how many of your deeds matched your words, but will ask how many times they didn't.

17. God won't ask how many books you read, but will ask how many people understood the Bible better by reading you.

18. God won't ask what college you attended, but will ask how you used your education to serve.

19. God won't ask where you shopped, but will ask who you shopped for.

20. God won't ask what you drove, but will ask where your driving took you. (NB: I am unfamiliar with the beliefs of the Chaldeans and I am not endorsing them or their beliefs in any way by citing the "20 things God won't ask on judgment day" that I came across on their website.)

If you haven't read Rick Warren's book *The Purpose Driven Life*, you need to. It helps one focus on the real and true priorities of Christians. We are made to serve Him and others. JOY= Jesus, others, you. We need to seek God continually as to what He wants to accomplish in our lives. We need to be willing to give Him our all: our talents, our time, everything for His glory. As Warren reminds us, our mission is to spread the gospel. Ask God to use you to witness to others and to give you a burden for the lost.

What then is your level of involvement in ministry? Are you regularly involved in at least one ministry at your church or in your community? Have you invested yourself through mentoring in the personal or ministry development of at least one other person in the past six months? Have you witnessed to anyone recently? Have you invited anyone to a Christian event in the past three months, such as a church service, Christian concert, Alpha group (www.alphana.org)? Are you connected to a small group that emphasizes spiritual growth? Do you abide in Christ with regular personal devotions? Do you take advantage of opportunities to encourage others in ministry?

You need to identify your gifts and callings and then use them to minister to others and to further His Kingdom. If you are not being used in your local church in some capacity, find a need and fill it, whether it be helping to take up the collection, greeting visitors as they come in for a service, leading a group, teaching Sunday School—wherever help may be needed in any capacity.

If you go to http://buildingchurch.net/g2s.htm, you will find the Wagner–modified Houts Questionnaire to clarify what your gifts and callings may be.

Two more tests to determine your spiritual gifts online:
http://mintools.com/spiritual–gifts–test.htm
http://www.elmertowns.com/spiritual%5Fgifts%5Ftest/

DISCERNING GOD'S WILL
WHEN MAKING DECISIONS[9]

Dr. Bill Coleman provides the following questions to determine God's will.

First ask yourself:

1. Is there a Bible absolute about this, for example, "thou shalt not steal"?

2. Is there a biblical principle? (ie: we should earn a living)

3. Any biblical examples that apply by person or situation?

4. What godly advice am I receiving from other Christians?

5. Do I have peace with God about this?

6. Will this hinder or help my spiritual growth and service for Jesus? (Hebrews 12: 1)

7. Does this put Jesus and God first in my life?

8. What would Jesus Himself do?

9. Will this help me do good for others?

10. Will this benefit the whole family/everyone involved as a win–win situation?

11. Will this yoke me with an unbeliever?
    (2 Corinthians 6:14)

12. Will this help or harm my body? (2 Corinthians 5:1)

13. Does this use my body to glorify God?
    (1 Corinthians 6:19, 20)

14. Can this activity cause addictions?
    (1 Corinthians 6:12)

15. Am I fulfilling a lust of the flesh? (2 Timothy 2:22)

16. Does this send a wrong message to others?
    (1 Thessalonians 5:10–22)

17. Does this activity promote/hinder evangelism?
    (Colossians 4:5)

18. Am I putting my personal preferences ahead of my
    impact on other Christians? (Romans 12:16)

19. Does this build up or tear down other Christians?

DISCERNING TRUTH FROM ERROR[10]

J.B. Nicholson poses the following questions to discern truth from error.

With so many varied teachings being promoted by professing Christians, it is easy to get away from true biblical teaching. Any teaching, no matter who is giving it, can be tested with the following nine questions. If the answer is yes to any one of these questions you can be sure that the teaching is not sound, balanced doctrine.

1. Does it demean the person of Christ: His nature, His offices, or His work?

2. Does it elevate man apart from the cross work of Christ and the believer's standing in Christ?

3. Does it depend on an obscure verse or a forced interpretation?

4. Does it contradict the overall tenor of Scripture: God's person, provision, plan, people?

5. Does it unduly emphasize the role of the Holy Spirit?

6. Does it encourage wrong behaviours or elitist attitudes?

7. Does it confuse the role or purpose of Israel, the Kingdom, and the Church?

8. Does it focus our attention on the temporal rather than the eternal? On the material rather than the spiritual?

9. Is it a thinly disguised version of a contemporary secular trend?

If the teaching passes all of these tests, or if you are unsure if it does, then it is worthwhile to subject it to this final test, to which an answer of no is a strong warning to be careful: Is it believed by those whom you know to be walking with the Lord and are Christlike?

If God is speaking to us—in our spirit or through another person—His word will always support it in some way. The devil is the father of lies and often disguises himself as an angel of light. Ask: Is what I'm hearing causing me to doubt God's Word or believe His Word? If we doubt God's Word, it could be a clue that we are not hearing from God. When God asks us to do something, it is in a gentle way.

If we feel condemned over past sin, we need to declare that we've been forgiven and "our sins are forgotten as far as the east is from the west" (Psalm 103:12). It is written, "I am the righteousness of God in Christ Jesus. God loves me and accepts me. And I can do all things through Christ who strengthens me" (Philippians 4:13).

(Also, the Bible warns us not to add to Scripture, nor to revoke or remove it. Please be aware of this if you belong to a church where there is another book that is used in equal or superior standing to the sixty–six books of the Bible!—Revelation 22:18)

BEING LED BY THE HOLY SPIRIT

> Although the Lord gives you the bread of adversity and the water of affliction, your teachers will be hidden no more; with your own eyes you will see them. Whether you turn to the right or to the left, your ears will hear a voice behind you, saying, "This is the way; walk in it."
>
> Isaiah 30:20–21 (NIV)

The three best known ways that God leads His people through the Holy Spirit are with the inward witness, the inward voice, and the audible voice of the Lord. Very rarely does God speak out loud to us but it may happen. If you are ever alone and you hear a voice and find yourself turning around to see who spoke, you may have heard from the Lord Himself directly!

Most often, however, God speaks to our spirits, which is known as an "inward witness." "For as many as are led by the Sprit of God, they are the sons of God" (Romans 8:14). God also leads us by an inward voice that we think of as the "still small voice." It is a "knowing"—something we recognize as being more than our own thoughts. "I say the truth in Christ, I lie not, my conscience also bearing me witness in the Holy Spirit" (Romans 9:1).

Anytime you think you have heard from the Lord, however, you should always ensure that the message lines up with the Word of God. In 1 Thessalonians 5:21 we read, "Prove all things." The Bible acts as a sort of "lie detector" in this sense.

Part of the role of the Holy Spirit is to convict of sin (John 16:8). You may be about to say something you shouldn't to someone, for example, when you feel a tug in your spirit to hold off saying something that would offend the other party— almost like the Lord tapping you on the shoulder to remind you to be kind to others.

God can speak through His Holy Spirit to us through His Word as well. I am sure you have noticed when reading the Bible that occasionally a verse or passage will seem to jump right off the page at you and you have a "Eureka" moment; you realize that God is speaking directly to you through that text and it was just what you needed to hear for that time or situation.

God can even use a non–Christian book or a TV show or a movie or another person to get a message across to us. It could be an answer to prayer that we have been seeking or it could be more of a confirmation message about something or it could be something God wants you to have greater understanding about and, sometimes, He just wants to commune with us.

God may want to warn of us some impending danger, and therefore, His voice may seem authoritative and stern; however, usually if you are hearing from God, you will not feel fear or apprehension. "I will hear what God the Lord will speak: for he will speak peace unto his people, and to his saints: but let them not turn again to folly" (Psalm 85:8).

Be prepared; maintain a listening ear at all times so that God can direct you easily as you carry out your routine daily activities. You know how frustrating it is when you are trying to reach someone, only to find that their cell phone is turned off; make sure you are "in tune" and in "receive mode" with the Holy Spirit at all times.

Discerning God's Voice

Dean Van Druff[11] offers the following advice on how to discern God's voice.

Outside of miraculous visitations and audible voices, our general problem is one of hearing God's "still small voice." What would the Spirit have us do next? This leadership comes through "promptings" to our hearts or minds, which are generally low–risk until we mature. God tells us to call someone late at night; to give someone the money in our pocket; to offer to pray with someone about something very specific that we couldn't have known. Often, we'll go wrong, but if we humbly reflect on our errors we can gain confidence for future promptings.

The problem is that we are on a hostile channel. Our minds can be prompted by God from our own carnal desires or from unclean spirits. Some ignore this and naively believe that anything they think or feel is from God, without humility or reflection. Beyond demonic promptings, our routine problem is the flesh. We want to look spiritual, we covet something, we want to defend ourselves. These often get blamed on God, and acted upon.

> The man who enters by the gate is the shepherd of his sheep.
> The watchman opens the gate for him, and the sheep listen
> to his voice. He calls his own sheep by name and leads them
> out. When he has brought out all his own, he goes on ahead of

them, and his sheep follow him because they know his voice. But they will never follow a stranger; in fact, they will run away from him because they do not recognize a stranger's voice.

John 10:2–5 (NIV)

If we have learned to discern God's voice in small things by acting on God's low–risk promptings and finding them validated with fruit that lasts, then God may prompt us to "tell that person I am going to heal them." At this point of maturity, those practiced at knowing God's voice need not pretend or merely hope. They can speak with authority, conviction, and results (Romans 12:2). They need not be double–minded or resort to psychological gymnastics (James 1:5–8). They can pray in real faith (James 5:15). For "faith comes by hearing, and hearing by the word of God" (Romans 10:17).

Obeying the Father's Voice

Often we ask God to speak to us, only to hear back, "If you are so interested in what I think, then why didn't you do the last thing I told you?" Obedience is the response that keeps the dialogue going. If we refuse to do what God tells us in the little things, we risk deafening our spiritual ear. If we refuse to do what God speaks in the big things, we risk his active rebuke.

But they refused to pay attention; stubbornly they turned their backs and stopped up their ears. They made their hearts as hard as flint and would not listen…So the Lord Almighty was very angry. "When I called, they did not listen; so when they called, I would not listen,' says the Lord Almighty."

Zechariah 7:11–13 (NIV)

Imagine your own son coming to you in great earnestness and saying, "Father, please speak to me. What would you have me do?" You respond, "I would like you to clean your room." Thrilled at the sound of your voice, the child goes off elated, but does not clean the room. Later, he approaches again, "Father, please disclose your will to your humble child." You tell him again, "Go clean your room." Pleased, he withdraws himself again, but does not do what you asked. Yet again, your son comes to you, "Oh great Father, I long to do your bidding! Grant me the favor of your wisdom and direction." What would you do at this point? "Do not merely listen to the word, and so deceive yourselves. Do what it says" (James 1:22, NIV). In other words, pray then obey! Make sure you have no unconfessed sin in your life. Be open to receiving God's leading in any way, shape, or form.

Resources:

Hearing God: developing a conversational relationship with God by Dallas Willard

Hearing God by Peter Lord—The author explains the many ways God, through the Holy Spirit, speaks to us.

FORGIVENESS IS ESSENTIAL

The importance of forgiving people who have hurt you cannot be too strongly emphasized. Not only is this a biblical command but it is essential for healing and if you are to move forward. "But if ye forgive not men their trespasses, neither will your father forgive your trespasses" (Matthew 6:15).

We need to remind ourselves that Jesus died for their sins as well as ours. The person who wronged you will be judged by God. Romans 12:19 admonishes us in this way: "Dearly beloved, avenge not yourselves, but rather give place unto wrath: for it is written, Vengeance is mine; I will repay, saith the Lord."

So forgiveness, then, is more for our benefit, for our peace and health and well-being. When we carry resentment, it affects us physically, psychologically, and spiritually. It also affects our relationship with God and others.

It is like swallowing poison and we can develop roots of bitterness that the Bible warns against (Hebrews 12:15). Often you hear there may be a connection between unforgiveness and diseases like cancer or rheumatoid arthritis. Studies have shown that holding a grudge can cause an excessive release of stress hormones (a factor in heart disease) and a weakening of the parasympathetic nervous system and immune system.[12]

If we don't forgive someone who has hurt us, then we remain their victims and they continue to have power over us.

We are still allowing them to hurt us by hurting ourselves with resentment. When we forgive them, we set ourselves free from their influence over us so that we can move on and have peace in our hearts and minds.

The first step in forgiving others is to make a decision to forgive. You won't "feel" like forgiving someone who has deeply wounded you. Choose to be obedient to God by forgiving others and then ask God to do the work in your heart that needs to be done to complete the act of forgiveness.

It helps if you can develop some pity or compassion for the person who has wronged you. If you can try to imagine why they are they way they are or if you can try to understand why they behaved that way toward you, you can often begin to see the person in a different light. That doesn't mean excusing or condoning wrong, sinful, or hurtful behaviour. When we forgive, we are not saying that it is okay that the person acted that way. It is not likely that we will forget a very hurtful incident either, but we don't have to allow ourselves to continue to be affected by the memory. (Forgiveness of abuse is covered in the chapter "Effects of Abuse.")

It might help to do mental imagery exercises if you are still having trouble forgiving someone. You can picture the person who offended you as being in a deep, dark dungeon in a locked cell. Then visualize yourself standing in front of the cell with the key in your hand that can free them. Choose to let them out and let them go by opening the lock and opening the door. You might even have to picture yourself locked in the cell with the key to see that you are the one that is not free if you haven't forgiven others. How long will you choose to remain there when you have the means to be free?

Here is an exercise that can help you to overcome painful memories; however, be aware that in recalling the hurtful incident, you may be flooded with negative emotions before the healing is complete.

Working Through Painful Memories:

Step 1

Pick a time when you know there will be no distractions for at least an hour and you have time to be alone. Be prepared for negative feelings and emotions to surface.

Step 2

Pray that God will direct you in recalling the memories you need to heal and to take you to the source of the distress and to the root of underlying emotions. Sometimes it helps if you ask yourself when is the first time you felt any negative emotion, such as shame or rejection or worthlessness, and try to recall the very first memory associated with that emotion.

Step 3

Recall a specific incident that resulted in you feeling hurt or rejected or another intense negative emotion. Try to engage all your senses of sight, smell, taste, sound, and touch to recapture the memory. Acknowledge how you felt in that situation at the time. For example, someone shared a memory of when they were around five or six years old. His mother tried to wash a birthmark off his arm. The child felt rejected in that his own mother did not even know her own child well enough to know that the mark on his arm was not dirt but a birthmark that had always been there. The mother insisted in washing it off and rubbed and rubbed until the child's arm was almost raw. Of course, the mark was still there.

The underlying emotions associated with this incident were that the child felt that the mother couldn't really love him if she didn't even know her own child's body. He felt rejected, unloved by his mother, and unlovable in general. Allow yourself to feel the painful emotions of the memory you are recalling. Name the emotions. Describe how you felt and the thoughts that were going through your head at the time.

Step 4

Recognize any lies associated with the memory. In our example, the little boy believed that he must be bad or unlovable if his own mother did not love him. He mistakenly assumed that if his own mother could not or did not love him, then no one else ever could. He felt insignificant and worthless and concluded that there must be something wrong with him. (Children aren't usually able to comprehend that the parent may actually be the one with the problem.)

Step 5

Often, at this time, it is helpful to visualize a loving Jesus being there in that moment in time, allowing the situation but feeling great empathy for what was happening to the child. Some people prefer to imagine their present day friends and supportive family members surrounding them at that moment telling them the truth. In our example they might be saying things like, "You are loved, we love you, you are special, we know that is a birthmark, this does not in any way make you a less lovable person." Other people might want to imagine their "adult self" with their "child self" saying the same kinds of affirmations. You can picture these people or your "adult self" hugging the child, wiping away his tears, loving him.

Step 6

Choose to believe the truth and not the lies developed from this memory. Receive the love of God. He allowed this incident to happen for a good and loving reason. Accept that. If you have held this incident/memory against God, forgive Him now (even though He needs no forgiveness). Remind yourself of God's love for you. (Read "Father's Love Letter in the chapter "Accepting God's Love.")

Step 7

Choose to forgive the person who hurt you. In our example, the person needed to forgive his mother. Sometimes it helps if you think of reasons why you should have sympathy for that person (ie: she had mental health issues, she didn't know better, she was drinking.). Know that if you don't forgive that person, you will continue to be their victim because unforgiveness causes us to be bitter and then we hurt ourselves, are robbed of peace, and are kept from being right with God. If it is difficult, tell God you are willing to be obedient by choosing to forgive, but that you need Him to help make your feelings match that decision. Forgive with the agape love of God.

Sometimes it helps if you write the person a letter without intending to give it to them. You could say how you felt and all the ways that incident has affected you in your life since: affected your self–esteem, relationships, not taking risks, etc. Describe all the losses it meant for you. Then, destroy the letter.

You could use that visualization I mentioned imagining that person locked in a cell in a dungeon and only you have the key. Picture yourself going down to their cell and them looking pathetic. Remember that Jesus died for their sins too. Open the door and let them out. If that doesn't work, picture yourself locked in the cell because you are in a prison of unforgiveness. Choose to free yourself by forgiving them.

Step 8

Now, as an adult, affirm the truths of that memory about yourself out loud. "I am lovable. God loves me. God knows everything about me, etc." Reinforce these affirmations with Bible verses that speak of God's love for you.

Step 9

Ask God to heal the memory and underlying emotions and to help you overcome the lies once and for all. Commit the memory to God and release it to Him. Pray to be able to receive His love and to be able love and accept yourself. Choose to let go of the past and live in the present.

You may have seen the following story in an e-mail forward written by Marion Bell.[13] She tells of a young lady named Sally and her teacher Dr. Smith. In one of her classes. Dr. Smith asked his students to draw a picture of someone that they disliked or someone who had made them angry. He then gave them permission to throw darts at the person's picture. Everyone was able to think of someone who had hurt them. The class lined up and began tossing the darts at the targets, some with a great deal of force and anger. Then the teacher began to remove the target from the wall and revealed a picture of Jesus underneath. As the students looked at the holes and rips covering his face and his pierced eyes, Dr. Smith said, "Inasmuch as ye have done it unto the least of these my brethren, ye have done it unto Me" (Matthew 25:40).

Forgiveness

To forgive
Is not to forget.
To forgive
Is really to remember
That nobody is perfect
That each of us stumbles
When we want so much to stay upright
That each of us says things
We wish we had never said

That we can all forget that love
Is more important than being right. To forgive is really to
remember
That we are so much more
Than our mistakes
That we are often more kind and caring
That accepting another's flaws
Can help us accept our own.

To forgive is to remember
That the odds are pretty good that
We might soon need to be forgiven ourselves.
That life sometimes gives us more
Than we can handle gracefully.

To forgive is to remember
That we have room in our hearts to
Begin again
And again,
And again.
And again.[14]

Of course, our best example of forgiveness is Jesus Himself on the Cross when He uttered, "Father, forgive them, they know not what they do" (Luke 23:34).

Prayer:

"Father, I choose to let go of all bitterness and resentment of any kind. I ask that you forgive and release all who have wronged and hurt me (name those people, organizations that come to mind) I purpose to walk in love and to seek peace with others. Thank you that your love is shed abroad in my heart by the Holy Ghost which is given to me." (Romans 5:5)

Resources:

The Peacemaker by Ken Sande—
Christians Resolving Conflict.

HINDRANCES TO ANSWERED PRAYER

There are many biblical explanations for unanswered prayer. As mentioned earlier, however, all prayers are heard and answered (John 16:24). Here are some reasons why the answer to your prayer could be "no" or "not yet."

Never Received Christ as Saviour

"He who belongs to God hears what God says. The reason you do not hear is that you do not belong to God" (John 8:47). His sheep hear His voice (John 10:3). If you haven't accepted that Jesus died in your place on the Cross for your sins, then now is the time to do that to ensure a right relationship with God. Receive the free gift of salvation and surrender your life to Him.

Doubt

Notice in Matthew 21:22, Jesus said, "*If* you believe, you will receive whatever you ask for in prayer. James affirms this, "But when he asks, he must believe and not doubt, because he who doubts is like a wave of the sea, blown and tossed by the wind. That man should not think he will receive anything from the Lord; he is a double-minded man, unstable in all he does" (James 1:6–8). Doubt is a serious obstacle to spiritual growth. If this is a problem area for you, find out what is at the root of it: trust issues from your childhood? Not truly believing God's love for you? Not believing that He has your best interest at heart? Not yielding to His sovereignty?

Wrong Motives

Jeremiah 17: 9 reminds us of how deceitful our own hearts can be, "When you ask, you do not receive, because you ask with wrong motives, that you may spend what you get on your pleasures." So examine your heart when you go to pray and try to pray in a way that would benefit everyone involved (James 4:3). Or we might have the right motives, but God has a much better way of answering a certain prayer—I am so thankful that God knows best and that He doesn't always answer in the manner that we think is best. Always pray as Jesus did, "Nevertheless not my will, but thine, be done" (Luke 22:42).

Unconfessed Sin

Unconfessed sin affects our fellowship with God. "Surely the arm of the Lord is not too short to save, nor His ear too dull to hear. But your iniquities (sins) have separated you from God; your sins have hidden His face from you so that He will not hear" (Isaiah 59:1–2). To ensure that there are no hindrances in your relationship with God, do regular self-assessments and name/confess any sinful thoughts, attitudes, or behaviour that comes to mind. "If I regard iniquity in my heart, the Lord will not hear me" (Psalm 66:13).

Habitual Sin

What if we have confessed our sins, but fall into the sin–confess–sin cycle? We are told in 2 Chronicles 7:14, "*If* they pray to me and *repent* and turn away from the evil they have been doing, *Then* I will hear them in heaven, forgive their sins, and make their land prosperous again." Perhaps you have been involved in some sin that you continue in, all the while deceiving yourself that everything is okay between you and God and that He will answer your prayers. It is one thing that we are not perfect and that we will fail; however, if there is something that we know we need to overcome once and for all, then God expects us to do whatever is necessary to get the victory in that area of our lives.

Idolatry

"Son of man, these men have set up idols in their hearts and put wicked stumbling blocks before their faces. Should I let them inquire of me at all?"(Ezekiel 14:3). Idols come in so many forms—it could be money or your career or your spouse or even wanting a spouse more than God's will. Anything that has control over you or that you give your time to more than you do in your relationship to God could be a potential idol in your life. Make sure your priorities are pleasing to Him.

Refusal to Help the Poor

Job is our example of how God wants us to view those less fortunate. "Did not I weep for him that was in trouble? Was (not) my soul grieved for the poor?" (Job 30:25). In fact, we are told in Proverbs that there will be troubles for those who do not help the needy, "He that giveth unto the poor shall not lack: but he that hideth his eyes shall have many a curse" (Proverbs 28:27). In regards to answered prayer, Proverbs 21:13 reminds us, "If a man shuts his ears to the cry of the poor, he too will cry out and not be answered."

Not Abiding in Him and His Word

"*If* you remain in me and my word remains in you, ask whatever you wish and it will be given to you" (John 15:7). Again, notice the *if* here; there is a condition with the promise. What does it mean to abide in Him? To endure without yielding, to bear patiently, to accept without objection, to remain stable or fixed. "He shall not be afraid of evil tidings: his heart is fixed, trusting in the Lord" (Psalm 12:7).

Unforgiveness

The Bible is very clear that we cannot be in a right relationship with God if we are holding a grudge or resentment in our hearts toward others. "For *if* you forgive men when they sin against you, your heavenly Father will also forgive you. But *if* you do not forgive men their sins, your Father will not forgive your sins" (Matthew 6:14–15, NIV).

Jesus declared in Mark 11:25–26, "And when ye stand praying, forgive, if ye have ought against any: that your Father also which is in heaven may forgive you your trespasses. But if ye do not forgive, neither will your Father which is in heaven forgive your trespasses" (KJV).

Unresolved Marital Issues

Martial relationships are specifically mentioned in 1 Peter 3:7 where husbands are admonished to "Treat them (their wives) with respect, because they also will receive, together with you, God's gift of life. Do this so that nothing will interfere with your prayers."

Unresolved Conflict with Others

God wants us to come before Him knowing that we are in a right relationship with both Him and others (vertically and horizontally, if you will). "So if you are about to offer your gift to God at the altar and there you remember that your brother has something against you, leave our gift there in front of the altar, go at once and make peace with your brother, and then come back and offer your gift to God" (Matthew 5:23–24).

Vain Repetitions

In Matthew 6:7 Jesus said, "When you pray, do not use a lot of meaningless words, as the pagans do, who think that God will hear them because their prayers are long." Isn't it odd that when some people pray in front of others they start speaking in Old English terms sometimes? Or it sounds as though they are trying to impress others instead of speaking to God from their heart like they do when they are at home alone and in need? Simple conversation with reverence for who God is suffice.

Judgmental or Critical Attitude

We are warned in James 4: 6 that "God opposes the proud but gives grace to the humble" (James 4:6, NIV). Luke 6: 37, "Judge not, and ye shall not be judged: condemn not, and ye shall not be condemned."

Not Doing Your Part

God is always willing and able to help us in our need; however, we should always do whatever we can to help ourselves. You can't expect to pray for employment, for example, and then not do a job search or not go to job interviews. You can't expect God to help you overcome a habit if you are not doing whatever you can to overcome it as well. When Simon Peter went fishing, he may have prayed that the Lord would supply fish, but he was still responsible for obeying Jesus' specific command to cast the net on the right side of the boat and then he still had to get all the fish into the boat and transport it (John 21:6). So, when you pray, see if there is any step of obedience you should be taking and ask God what you can do or ask Him to show what you can do, if anything.

Collective Prayer

God answers prayers that are prayed alone; however, we are told in Matthew 18:19, "If two of you shall agree on earth as touching any thing that they shall ask, it shall be done for them of my Father which is in heaven," and in Ecclesiastes 4:12, it says, "A threefold cord is not quickly broken." Even Jesus asked his disciples to watch and pray with Him in his greatest hour of need (Matthew 26:38).

Fasting with Prayer

In Matthew 17, the disciples asked Jesus why they could not cast a demon out of a boy and Jesus spoke to them of their unbelief and then added, "Howbeit this kind goeth not out but by prayer and fasting."

Ingratitude

We are told in 1 Thessalonians 5:16–18 to "Be joyful always, pray at all times, be thankful in all circumstances. This is what God wants from you in your union with Christ Jesus." Notice that prayer is mentioned in between being joyful and being thankful. Are you being obedient in this respect? Regardless of what prayers are seemingly not yet answered in our lives, there are all kinds of things to be thankful for, every day.

Lack of Persistence

Jesus told the parable of the widow who kept pleading for her rights to a corrupt judge (Luke 18:1–8). He eventually granted her requests just to be free of her. Jesus gave another example of persistence in prayer in Luke 11:5–8. A man went to a friend's house at midnight to borrow some bread. Jesus points out that even if the friend won't get up and give him bread because of their friendship, he will give him bread because he keeps on asking. I know a woman who prayed for thirty years for her husband's salvation and he finally accepted Christ as His

Saviour. If you have any long–standing prayers, don't give up; however, it may be helpful to ask God if you should be praying differently about it or whether you should stand in faith and confess the result though not yet seen.

Spiritual Opposition

In Daniel 10:1–14, we read of the account of the angel telling Daniel that although God heard his prayer the moment it was spoken, he was delayed by twenty–one days due to spiritual opposition.

Timing

A great example of this is in Luke 1:11–20. Zechariah had prayed for a son. It was a prayer that had seemingly gone unheard or unanswered; however, many years later, when it would seem impossible, his request was granted!

Not Praying in Accordance with God's Will or His Word

"This is the confidence we have in approaching God: that if we ask anything according to His will, He hears us" (1 John 5:14, NIV). Sometimes we just don't pray according to God's will or we are praying for something contrary to God's Word. When Jesus was in the Garden of Gesthemane, He said, "Not my will but thine be done" (Luke 22:42). We are encouraged to bring all our requests to God but we should also add that it be " according to His will" and that it be in the best interests of everyone involved. It wouldn't hurt to add something like "and help me to accept the answer to my prayer even if it is not answered in the way that I expect or in my timing."

Not Recognizing an Answer to Prayer

Sometimes God answers our prayer in a way that we don't recognize because of our limited, earthly understanding. God is "all knowing" and can see things that we can't. He can also see how everything is working together for His purposes and He knows just the right timing. We need to learn to trust God rather than our own understanding of what's best for us. "Trust in the Lord with all your heart and lean not on your own understanding; in all ways acknowledge Him, and He will make your paths straight" (Proverbs 3:5–6). "For my thoughts are not your thoughts, neither are your ways my ways declared the Lord. As the heavens are higher than the earth, so are my ways higher than your ways and my thoughts higher than your thoughts" (Isaiah 55:8–9).

We are given the assurance in 1 Corinthians 13:12 that we now see things dimly, as in a mirror (in those days the mirrors were made out of metal and not too clear apparently), but someday we will see clearly and understand how God answered our prayers.

Sometimes God may not answer a prayer because it would mean overriding a previous prayer. For example, if we pray for patience and then we are allowed trials and tribulations so that God can develop that patience in us, why should He then answer the prayer to be delivered from all our trials? In that case, the latter prayer would be at cross purposes with the first prayer and God will always answer according to His higher purposes.

Be careful what you pray for; if you pray for unshakeable faith or tell God that you are willing to experience longsuffering for His sake, be prepared for events that will challenge your faith.

Focus on answered prayer. Some people are so focused on unanswered prayer that they totally discount all the answers to prayer they do receive. It may be helpful to keep a prayer journal to record answers to prayer, even though they may be in a different form or at a different time than expected.

Most people know when they buy a house, that at some point they will have repairs to do or upgrading. At the very least, they will have to maintain the property's current condition; however, these hindrances need not deter anyone from appreciating the good things about owning a home.

In the same way, hindrances to prayer should be dealt with accordingly. The reward of having a close relationship with God and trusting Him to hear and answer your prayers is worth it. Whenever it appears as though God has not answered your prayer, you have to choose to believe that He is still a good and loving God who always answers prayer in His way and His timing according to His good and loving reasons that are always in our best interest.

IT'S ALL ABOUT ATTITUDE

I tell my counseling clients that life is 5% of what happens to them and 95% of how they respond to what happens to them. I am sure you have heard clichés like "Turn lemons into lemonade" or "Play the hand that you are dealt." The fact is that, as Christians, we are required to live above our circumstances. We can expect troubles in our lives and as someone has said, "God is more concerned with our holiness than with our happiness."

This does not mean that God doesn't care how we feel or that He doesn't want us to be happy. He wants us to have the "joy of the Lord," which is the peace and comfort of knowing we have His help despite whatever we are going through. We can go through trying times grumbling and complaining or we can keep our focus positive and grounded in His word. Chances are that the trial will last much longer until we are willing to change our attitudes.

The key is to choose to believe that God is a good and loving God who always allows bad things to happen in our lives for a good and loving reason. If we truly understand God's character (holy and just) and His nature (love), and if we believe His word is true, then we know that He has a good plan for us and that He is working everything out for good in our lives (Romans 8:28).

Think of baking a cake, you wouldn't want to eat flour on its own or baking soda by itself or a raw egg, but you put all those ingredients together and you can make a delicious tasting cake. It is the same way with everything going on in our lives. Events or circumstances on their own may be quite distasteful and difficult to swallow, but the end result will be something good for us and for others.

Another analogy is the one of the tapestry. If you look at the back of such a piece of work, you see all the threads and tangles and knots and disorder but if you look at the front of a finished piece, you see everything has been woven together perfectly to make something beautiful and special. We have to trust that God's ways and thoughts really are higher than ours (Isaiah 55:9).

Even if we were called upon to suffer our whole lives on this earth, we would need to trust that something good is being accomplished according to His plan and purposes. For some people, this is what motivates them to think about what heaven is like and to yearn for their time there with God. In his book *God is Not Fair*, Joel Freeman states that the highest form of love is to continue to love God even when He doesn't alleviate the suffering in your life.

It is hard for us to grasp but this life is really only a hiccup in the face of eternity or as someone once described it: as one word within an entire book.

How do we change our perspective then? By renewing the mind as stated in Romans 12:2. This means retraining our thinking. The mind is like a room that has been wallpapered with ugly wallpaper (negative beliefs about oneself, the world, the future, others). Essentially, you need to re–wallpaper the walls of your mind with positive thinking but not just positive thinking, with the truth, which is the Word of God.

The way to internalize this truth is to eat it, breathe it, sleep it or, if you will, "become one with the word." Memorize as many Bible verses as you can, but not just any verses, make sure they are verses that specifically counteract the areas of your thinking patterns that are particularly negative or troublesome.

For every doubt thought, quote a faith verse. For every fear thought, replace it with a verse about God's provision or protection or about Him empowering us. This takes consistent practice but when you change your thinking, your behaviour and your feelings will change as well.

In psychology, cognitive therapy can be effective for treating mood disorders such as anxiety and depression. As Christians, we have an even better answer: don't just replace negative thinking with a positive outlook, but replace it with the Word of God, which is life and truth. We can cry because roses have thorns or we can celebrate that thorns have roses.

If you notice in Ephesians where it mentions the armor of God, the only offensive weapon is the Sword of the Spirit. All the rest, like the helmet of salvation and breastplate of righteousness, are defensive weapons. When Jesus was in the wilderness for forty days, every time the devil tempted him, Jesus began his response with, "It is written…" and then quoted scripture. That should be our response as well when tempted to doubt or despair.

People develop negative thinking patterns from childhood based on core beliefs. For example, if a child was abused he/she might develop the following negative core beliefs: "The world is not a safe place" or "I am bad, there must be something wrong with me that I am treated this way" or "I am not loved or valued and never will be" or "People cannot be trusted" and so forth. These core beliefs are what we revert to as adults years later time and time again whenever we feel vulnerable, threatened, rejected, or insecure.

These core beliefs must also be replaced by the truth, which is the Word of God. Here are some examples of how to counteract negative thinking and false core beliefs.

Why Should I Say I Can't?

The following verses were compiled by Dr. Bill Coleman[15]

1. Why should I say I can't when the Bible says I can do all things through Christ who gives me strength? (Philippians 4:13)

2. Why should I worry when I know that God will take care of all my needs according to His riches in glory in Christ Jesus? (Philippians 4:19)

3. Why should I fear when the Bible says God has not given me a spirit of fear, but of power, love, and a sound mind? (2 Timothy 1:7)

4. Why should I lack faith to live for Christ when God has given me a measure of faith? (Romans 12:3)

5. Why should I be helpless when the Bible says the Lord is my strength of my life? (Psalm 27:1)

6. Why should I allow Satan control over my life when He that is in me is greater than he that is in the world? (1 John 4:4)

7. Why should I accept defeat when the Bible says that God always leads me in victory? (2 Corinthians 2:14)

8. Why should I lack wisdom when the Bible says that God gives me wisdom generously when I ask Him for it? (James 1:5)

9. Why should I be depressed when I can recall to mind God's lovingkindness, compassion, and faithfulness? (Lamentations 3:21–23)

10. Why should I worry and be upset when I can cast all my anxieties on Christ who cares for me? (1 Peter 5:7)

11. Why should I ever be in bondage when I know that there is freedom where the Spirit of the Lord is? (Galatians 5:1)

12. Why should I feel condemned when the Bible says there is no condemnation for those who are in Christ Jesus? (Romans 8:1)

13. Why should I feel alone when Jesus said He is with me always and will never leave me nor forsake me? (Matthew 28:20, Hebrews 13:5)

14. Why should I be unhappy when I, like Paul, can learn to be content whatever the circumstances? (Philippians 4:11)

15. Why should I feel worthless when Christ became sin for me so that I might become the righteousness of God? (2 Corinthians 5:21)

16. Why should I feel helpless when I know that if God is for me, who can be against me? (Romans 8:31)

17. Why should I feel like a failure when I am more than a conqueror through Christ who loves me? (Romans 8:37)

18. Why should I feel confused when God is the author of peace? (1 Corinthians 2:12)

19. Why should I let the pressures of life bother me when I can take courage knowing that Jesus has overcome the world? (John 16:33)

20. Why should I feel like I am cursed with bad luck when the Bible says that Christ rescued me from the curse of the law that I might receive His spirit by faith? (Galatians 3:13–14)

Philippians 4:8, "In conclusion, my brothers, fill your minds with those things that are good and that deserve praise: things that are true, noble, right, pure, lovely, and honorable."

JOY ROBBERS

Dr. Bill Coleman provided the following headings on topics that will steal your joy and hinder your spiritual growth. [16]

Jesus promised His followers that they could experience the same joy that He possessed. (John 15:11). The Bible warns us, however, that there are things that can rob us of this joy. The following list is quite extensive, but you may think of others.

Not Understanding our Identity in Christ:
Living Like a Poor Victim, Not a Victor
with God's power to Succeed:

It's amazing how many Christians have not been able to grasp who they really are in Christ Jesus. To know Him personally is to have access to Him, to His power, His love, His victory, His truth, His courage, etc. Romans 8:11 declares, "But if the Spirit of Him that raised up Jesus from the dead dwell in you, He that raised up Christ from the dead shall also quicken your mortal bodies by his Spirit that dwelleth in you." It's the same spirit dwelling within us that resurrected Jesus from death!

The best way to truly understand who you are in Christ is to read the following statements based on specific Bible verses, but read them out loud, with conviction, several times over until you start to really appreciate what it all means.

Who I am In Christ by Neil T. Anderson[17]

- I am a child of God (John 1:12).

- I have peace with God (Romans 5:1).

- The Holy Spirit lives in me (1 Corinthians 3:16).

- I have access to God's wisdom (James 1:5).

- I am helped by God (Hebrews 4:16).

- I am reconciled to God (Romans 5:11).

- I am not condemned by God (Romans 8:1).

- I am justified (Romans 5:1).

- I have Christ's righteousness (Romans 5:19; 2 Corinthians 5:21).

- I am Christ's ambassador (2 Corinthians 5:20).

- I am completely forgiven (Colossians 1:14).

- I am tenderly loved by God (Jeremiah 31:3).

- I am the sweet fragrance of Christ to God (2 Corinthians 2:15).

- I am a temple in which God dwells (1 Corinthians 3:16).

- I am blameless and beyond reproach (Colossians 1:22).

- I am the salt of the earth (Matthew 5:13).

- I am the light of the world (Matthew 5:14).

- I am a branch on Christ's vine (John 15:1,5).

- I am Christ's friend (John 15:5).

- I am chosen by Christ to bear fruit (John 15:6).

- I am a joint heir with Christ, sharing his inheritance with him (Romans 8:17).

- I am united to the Lord, one spirit with Him (1 Corinthians 6:17).

- I am a member of Christ's body (1 Corinthians 12:27)

- I am a saint (Ephesians 1:1).

- I am hidden with Christ in God (Colossians 3:3).

- I am chosen by God, holy and dearly loved (Colossians 3:12).

- I am a child of the light (1 Thessalonians 5:5).

- I am holy, and I share in God's heavenly calling (Hebrews 3:1).

- I am sanctified (Hebrews 2:11).

- I am one of God's living stones, being built up in Christ as a spiritual house (1 Peter 2:5).

- I am a member of a chosen race, a royal priesthood, a holy nation, a people for God's own possession and created to sing his praises (1 Peter 2:9–10).

- I am firmly rooted and built up in Christ (Colossians 2:7).

- I am born of God, and the evil one cannot touch me (1 John 5:18).

- I have the mind of Christ (1 Corinthians 2:16).

- I may approach God with boldness, freedom, and confidence (Ephesians 3:12).

- I have been rescued from Satan's domain and transferred into the kingdom of Christ (Colossians 1:13).

- I have been made complete in Christ (Colossians 2:10).

- I have been given a spirit of power, love, and self–discipline (2 Timothy 1:7).

- I have been given great and precious promises by God (2 Peter 1:4).

- My needs are met by God (Philippians 4:19).

- I am a prince (princess) in God's kingdom (John 1:12; 1 Timothy 6:15).

- I have been bought with a price, and I belong to God (1 Corinthians 6:19,20).

- I have been adopted as God's child (Ephesians 1:5).

- I have direct access to God through the Holy Spirit (Ephesians 2:18).

- I am assured that all things are working together for good (Romans 8:28).

- I am free from any condemning charges against me (Romans 8:31f).

- I cannot be separated from the love of God (Romans 8:35f).

- I have been established, anointed, and sealed by God (2 Corinthians 1:21,22).

- I am confident that the good work that God has begun in me will be completed (Philippians 1:6).

- I am a citizen of heaven (Philippians 3:20).

- I am a personal witness of Christ's (Acts 1:8).

- I am God's co–worker (2 Corinthians 6:1, 1 Corinthians 3:9).

- I am seated with Christ in the heavenly realm (Ephesians 2:6).

- I am God's workmanship (Ephesians 2:10).

- I can do all things through Christ, who gives me the strength I need (Philippians 4:13). [18]

Pessimistic, Negative Thinking/ Undisciplined Thought Life

We develop core beliefs about ourselves, others, and the world as children. Romans 12:2 tells us, "Be not conformed to this world: but be ye transformed by the renewing of your mind, that ye may prove what is that good, and acceptable, and per-fect, will of God."

The concept of retraining your thinking is covered in the chapter " It's All about Attitude." Pessimistic thinking also impacts our capacity for developing and maintaining faith. In Mark 9:24 we read the account of the father of the boy afflicted by evil spirits, "The father at once cried out, I do have faith, but not enough. Help me have more!" Pray for more faith but remember that we choose to believe that the Word of God is true. We choose to believe He is a loving God. We choose to believe His promises.

Satan is a thief who comes to rob God's Word from our minds. It is essential that we know how to win the battle of the mind by wearing the helmet of salvation and the full armor of God. (Ephesians 6:11–17). The sword of the spirit, which is the Word of God, is the only offensive weapon we have against the enemy. A spirit of fear can spiritually paralyze us; we need to counteract fear and doubt with verses like 2 Timothy1:7, "For God hath not given us a spirit of fear, but of power, and of love, and of a sound mind."

Second Corinthians 10:5 reminds us that we have a choice in what we allow ourselves to think, "Casting down imaginations, and every high thing that exalteth itself against the knowledge of God, and bringing into captivity every thought to the obedience of Christ." We can gain control over our thought life with consistent practice to change negative thinking patterns.

Unprocessed Grief and Loss Leading to Despair

This book has an entire chapter on grief and dealing with loss. If you feel you cannot cope with your loss alone, you don't have to; seek help. How do you know when you should seek professional help?

– When your physical health is affected because you are not eating enough or you are becoming ill often because your immune system is lowered.

– When you cannot carry out your normal, day–to–day activities.

– When you have isolated yourself from others to the point where you are alone most of the time and not even communicating with others on the phone.

— If you find yourself over–medicating or drinking excessively in an effort to deal with the pain.

Grief counselling is available through community resources,
churches, and licensed therapists. Join a grief support group;
local community papers will usually have listings. Use the
Internet and join an online bereavement support group dedicated to supporting individuals who have lost loved ones. www.
angel–on–my–shoulder.com is a good resource, for example.

Unresolved Conflict with Someone/
Disappointment with Someone

The Bible is very clear that if we want to be in a right relationship with God, then we need to be in a right relationship
with others. Unfortunately, it is not always non–Christians that
offend us. Christians can deeply wound other Christians. "And
when you stand and pray, forgive anything you may have against
anyone, so that your Father in heaven will forgive the wrongs
you have done" (Mark 11:25). Matthew 5:23 also admonishes
us to reconcile with others, "So if you are about to offer your
gift to God at the altar, go at once and make peace with your
brother, and then come back and offer your gift to God."

Matthew 18:15–17 gives us guidelines on how to resolve dis-
putes with other Christians,

> If your brother sins against you, go to him and show him his
> fault. But do it privately, just between yourselves. If he listens
> to you, you have won your brother back. But if he will not
> listen to you, take one or two other persons with you, so that
> every accusation may be upheld by the testimony of two or
> more witnesses, as the scripture says. And if he will not listen

to them, then tell the whole thing to the church. Finally, if he will not listen to the church, treat him as though he were a pagan or tax collector.

Read the chapter on forgiveness again if necessary. Unresolved sin against someone else will also hinder our relationship with God. If you have sinned against someone, you need to ask God's forgiveness and then try to make amends with that person. You will need to pray and ask God which sins you can just confess to Him and which ones require an action with that person. If you are not sure, read the chapter on "How to Make Decisions According to God's Will."

A Belief that We are Helpless and Trapped and There is no Way Out:

The Overwhelming Flood of Hopelessness and Despair

The principle of renewing our minds in Romans 12:2 is relevant here once again. (Refer to the chapter "It's All About Attitude.") We need to build ourselves up with the truth, which is the Word of God. Here are some examples of standing on the Word of God instead of giving in to negative thinking.

Why should I let the pressures of life bother me when I can take courage knowing that Jesus has overcome the world? (John 16:33)

Why should I feel helpless when I know that if God is for me, who can be against me? (Romans 8:31)

Why should I fear when the Bible says God has not given me a spirit of fear, but of power, and love, and a sound mind? (2 Timothy 1:7)

When you are feeling particularly "whipped," downtrodden or disillusioned, no matter how you feel, seek out support from other mature Christians: friends, family, or people from your church. Ask for prayer even if you have to call a prayer line or request prayer online from people you don't know. The chapter on "Overcoming Depression" lists symptoms of clinical depression. If you suspect you may be significantly depressed, see your family physician or a Christian psychiatrist (www.christiantherapist.com).

Unprocessed Trauma and Shock
Leading to Anxiety

An entire chapter is devoted to overcoming anxiety in this book; however, some Christians have experienced a trauma in their life that has resulted in Post–Traumatic Stress Disorder. Traumatic events causing PTSD could be: rape, combat exposure, childhood abuse/neglect, physical assault, being threatened with a weapon, natural disasters, bank robbery, hostage incidents, etc.

People have different emotional and psychological thresholds. About 20% of women go on to develop PTSD and about 8% of men. Available data suggests that approximately 30% of these individuals develop a chronic form that perpetuates throughout their lives. About 30 % of the men and women who have spent time in war zones experience PTSD.

Persistent symptoms that are indicative of PTSD are: nightmares, flashbacks, numbness of emotions, depression, anger, irritability, being easily startled. PTSD is treated by a variety of forms of psychotherapy and drug therapy. At present, cognitive–behavioural therapy appears to be somewhat more effective than drug therapy. However, it would be premature to conclude that drug therapy is less effective overall since drug trials for PTSD are at a very early stage. If you suspect that you have PTSD, it is important that you consult a professional to work through the memories of the trauma and receive healing so that the traumatic event will no longer impede your spiritual and emotional growth.

Resources:

http://www.ncptsd.va.gov/facts/index.html

Dealing with flashbacks: www.safehaven–uk.org/aftermath/panic.shtml

Lack of Self–Discipline

Perhaps it should be mandatory for all Christians to participate in some kind of Bible boot camp or basic training for Christians. Without self–discipline, one cannot carry out daily devotions, study the Word diligently, be obedient to God's commands, or renew one's thinking with the truth, which is the Word of God. To be self–disciplined, we need to take charge of our personal and spiritual growth. We need to decide that it is a priority in our lives and we need a concrete, structured plan to maintain our spiritual growth as something of utmost importance.

So it starts with a decision and a prayer. Ask God for a hunger and thirst after righteousness. Determine to be the best Christian you can be. If necessary, write down what that would take and then break it down into manageable steps.

If you are a morning person, schedule your devotions (Bible reading, prayer, and praise) in the morning before going off to work. If you are an evening person, have your devotions at night when you can be most focussed (although it is still important to start your day off by acknowledging God and asking for His leading first thing, even if for a few minutes). If you do not enjoy reading, obtain the Bible on DVD; there are new ones now that offer dramatizations and the Bible is on CDs as well, so if you are really busy and on the go, you can still listen to the Word in your car on the way to/from work.

If you are still having difficulty, ask someone to be your accountability partner, a friend or your spouse, to ensure that you keep working at it until you are more self–disciplined. You are the one who will lose out if you don't take responsibility for your spiritual growth.

Unbiblical Expectations from Life

Disappointment is often the result of unrealistic and/or unbiblical expectations. Sometimes there are consequences for sin even though forgiveness has been sought, genuine sorrow has been demonstrated, and the sin has not been repeated. David, the psalmist, was sorry for his adultery and for having his lover's husband, Uriah, killed. Even so, his son died. In fact, the Bible describes him as a "man after God's own heart" and yet he endured a dire consequence for his sinful behaviour.

We read about this in 2 Samuel 12:13–18,

> And David said unto Nathan, I have sinned against the Lord.
> And Nathan said unto David, The Lord also hath put away

thy sin; thou shalt not die. Howbeit, because by this deed thou hast given great occasion to the enemies of the Lord to blaspheme, the child also (that is)] born unto thee shall surely die. And Nathan departed unto his house. And the Lord struck the child that Uriah's wife bare unto David, and it was very sick. David therefore besought God for the child; and David fasted, and went in, and lay all night upon the earth. And the elders of his house arose, (and went) to him, to raise him up from the earth: but he would not, neither did he eat bread with them. And it came to pass on the seventh day, that the child died.

If someone has pre–marital sex, the consequences could be a pregnancy or a sexually transmitted disease. If someone commits a crime, one may have to complete a prison sentence. It is unrealistic to think that because one is saved by grace, that he is invincible, excluded from tragedy, or absolved from consequences as a result of his own actions.

There are natural laws—we know what happens if we try to defy gravity, for example. There are consequences if we do not adhere to biblical principles as well. Some people cannot grasp the idea that a loving God would allow people to go to hell. I like the analogy of the young girl who committed a driving offence. She stood before the judge, who happened to be her own father, and pled guilty. He looked down at her with love, and because of his love for her, he did not want to impose any suffering or hardship on her.

Yet, it was his job and his duty as the judge to carry out a penalty because she had clearly broken the law of the land. He fined her $1,000, but then he did an extraordinary thing—he took off his robe, got down from his seat, and paid the fine for his daughter. In the same way, God does not wish that any should perish or go to hell (2 Peter 3:9), so He sent His son as a way to pay for our penalties, our fines, our punishments. He is Holy and there must be consequences for breaking spiritual laws but because of His love for his own children, He paid the debt Himself through His son Jesus Christ.

Blocked Goals Leading to Anger

Everyone experiences blocked goals in life; it is always more important how you react to those blocked goals. I received an e–mail forward once that said you can tell someone's true character by how they handle life's little frustrations, like tangled Christmas lights. What about your reaction as a Christian to bad drivers out there? Then there are major blocked goals like not getting that job you wanted/needed, not finding the right mate, not being able to have children, and so forth.

In these situations, we always have to remind ourselves that Romans 8:28 rings true, "All things are working together for good for those who love God and are called according to his purpose." God is a good and loving God who always allows blocked goals for a good and loving reason.

We have to choose to believe that God has our best interests at heart and that we can trust in His love for us and in His higher plan for us. Isaiah 55:9, "For as the heavens are higher than the earth, so are my ways higher than your ways, and my thoughts than your thoughts." It might be helpful to read the chapter on anger management in part three of this book if you think this may still be a problem in your life.

Being Driven by Basic Longings

There is nothing wrong with basic longings. Everyone wants to have a sense of belonging and acceptance, to have financial security, comfort when feeling anxious or down, and so on. The problem may lie in where and how we seek to fulfill those longings. God had promised to meet all our needs (Philippians 4:19) and He wants us to look to Him. Romans 8:4 says, "That the righteousness of the law might be fulfilled in us, who walk not after the flesh, but after the Spirit."

If we rely on ourselves to meet our needs instead of depending on God, we can find ourselves struggling in sin or addictions. It is a form of pride as well to seek to meet our own needs through our own strength or in our own ways. Ask God to help you walk after the Spirit and to seek after His righteousness. We are encouraged in Matthew 6:31–35, "So do not start worrying: Where will my food come from? Or my drink? Or my clothes? These are the things the pagans are always concerned about. Your father in heaven knows that you need all these things. Instead, be concerned, above everything else, with the Kingdom of God and with what He requires of you, and He will provide you with all these other things."

Pray that your desires and God's desires for you will be the same so that your focus shifts from what you long for to what God wants for you and to what He requires of you. Our attitude should be that of one of His servants:

> Suppose one of you has a servant who is plowing or looking after the sheep. When he comes in from the field, do you tell him to hurry along and eat his meal? Of course not! Instead, you say to him, "Get my supper ready, then put on your

apron and wait on me while I eat and drink: after that you have your meal." The servant does not deserve thanks for obeying orders, does he? It is the same with you; when you have done all you have been told to do, say, "We are ordinary servants; we have only done our duty."

Luke 17:7–10

Instability Due to Lack of Clear Beliefs/Values

There is a clear difference between accepting Jesus as "Saviour" and accepting Him as "Lord" of your life. After I said the sinner's prayer and was told I needed to give God control of my life, I struggled for about six months with that decision. I was euphoric about getting to know God and feeling forgiven and having a new start in life, but give Him total control of my life? That was different!

Mark 12:30, "And thou shalt love the Lord thy God with all thy heart, and with all thy soul, and with all thy mind, and with all thy strength: this is the first commandment." Accepting Jesus as your Saviour is only the first step in many for Christians. It is absolutely essential to go forward in your Christian walk. That means to read the Bible and to really know God's Word by memorizing as many verses as possible and meditating on the Word. It means going to church and fellowshipping with other believers so we can support and encourage each other. It means consistent prayer. To be a Christian means to follow Christ and to follow His example, to emulate Him as much as possible.

Revelation 3:14–16 gave a warning to the church in Laodicea that is for us as well, "This is the message from the amen, the faithful and true witness, who is the origin of all that God has created. I know what you have done; I know that you are neither cold nor hot. How I wish you were either one or the other! But because you are lukewarm, neither hot nor cold, I am going to spit you out of my mouth!"

Not Living in Sync with our Beliefs/Values: Lack of Knowledge, Understanding, and/or Wisdom Leading to Confusion

You cannot be adhering to Christian beliefs/values if you don't even know what God requires of you because you don't read the Bible. Some people like to think of themselves as "spiritually eclectic," believing in elements of Christianity while believing in aspects of Buddhism and other religions at the same time. The Bible tells us, however, in John 14:9 that" if you have seen Jesus you have seen God." All other religions say they will lead you *to* the way, the truth, and the life. John 14:6, "Jesus saith unto him, I *am* the way, the truth, and the life: no man cometh unto the Father, but by me."

Others are professing Christians and yet they dabble in occult practices on a regular basis, such as playing Dungeons and Dragons or in astrology or fortune telling, all of which are anti–Christian activities and will impede spiritual growth. You cannot expect to experience the full blessings of the Lord if you are not committed to Him and His teachings. If you haven't surrendered your heart and life to God as of yet, do it today and see the difference it makes in your life.

"For God is not the author of confusion" (1 Corinthians 14:33).

Physiological Factors

There are organic causes for some conditions that affect our mood—diet, blood sugar, hormones, etc. Serotonin levels in the brain can contribute to depression and disorders, such as anxiety and obsessive compulsive disorders, and therefore, can be effectively treated with medication. I think it is always best to try everything else first before looking to medication; however, if nothing else has helped, then you need to see a physician. If the doctor prescribes medication, then you need to ensure that they monitor the dosage and the medication consistently. You may need to try different medications or change the dosage and you may need to wait four to six weeks before you see the results of some medications. Women can have their hormone levels tested by providing a blood sample to their physician.

First Corinthians 6:19 reminds us that "your body is the temple of the Holy Ghost which is in you, which ye have of God, and ye are not your own." If we don't take care of our bodies by getting enough sleep, recreation, adhering to a reasonable diet, exercise, and so forth, then we risk poor health by lowering our immune system and possibly making ourselves vulnerable to illnesses. We cannot be used for His glory to the best of our abilities if we are not in good condition physically, emotionally, and spiritually.

Theological Legalism

("I have to earn my salvation")

I can't imagine the frustration and despair one might experience if he truly believed that he had to earn his salvation and/or if he felt that he always had to measure up to please God. While I could cite countless scripture verses, including John 3:16, that explain that salvation is a free gift to all who receive it because God loved us, the fact is that it comes down to choosing to believe it. How could anyone possibly do enough good or be perfect enough to earn salvation anyway?

The truth is that there is nothing that you can do to make God love you any more or less than He does at this moment. Romans 8:35 explains how *nothing* can separate us from the love of Christ, "Who, then, can separate us from the love of Christ? Can trouble do it, or hardship or persecution or hunger or poverty or danger or death?" And verses 37–39, "No, in all these things we have complete victory through him who loved us! For I am certain that nothing can separate us from his love; neither death nor life, nor angels nor other heavenly rulers or powers, neither the present nor the future neither the world above nor the world below– there is nothing in all creation that will ever be able to separate us from the love of God which is ours through Jesus Christ our Lord."

That's quite a promise and we are assured in Galatians 2:16, "Knowing that a man is not justified by the works of the law, but by the faith of Jesus Christ, even we have believed in Jesus Christ, that we might be justified by the faith of Christ, and not by the works of the law: for by the works of the law shall no flesh be justified."

Debt and Inability to Pay the Debt

Being in debt is definitely an oppressive burden that weighs heavily on most people's shoulders. It is really easy to rack up credit card debt not realizing how much more you are actually paying and how long it will take to actually pay off the initial items plus the interest. Except for major purchases such as a house or car, it is a good idea not to put anything on a credit card unless you are going to pay it off totally each month. Your credit card company may reduce your interest rate or you may want to transfer the balance on a credit card to another company with a reduced interest charge. You can also consolidate your debts so that you have only one manageable payment a month.

www.crown.org is a Christian organization that may help you gain control over your spending. You may want to consult a financial advisor if you need help with budgeting and the sooner you can start preparing for retirement in the way of investments, the better.

If the problem is that your salary is not enough to meet your monthly expenses, then you need to change your lifestyle or set new career goals, even if that means getting training or going back to school.

There are all kinds of ways to help make ends meet: two single parents can share a house, for example, or you could take in a boarder. Brainstorm with people to come up with feasible solutions and then set short-and long-term goals for yourself. Break those goals down into manageable steps and get started with your first step. The government offers some paid training programs and there are employment agencies that specialize in helping disabled people or those over fifty with obtaining suitable employment.

Engaging in Sinful Behaviour/Activities

Jeremiah 17: 9 reminds us that "the heart is deceitful above all things, and desperately wicked: who can know it?" It is so easy to deceive ourselves into thinking we are right with God, even if we are involved in habitual sin. I am not talking about the little sins we commit from time to time as Christians because we are not perfect; we will never be perfect on earth. Read Galatians 5:19–21; let's not fool ourselves, we can be saved but our fellowship with God will be greatly affected if we are continually sinning. The chapter on habitual sin/addictions provides resources and further help with this topic.

Galatians 6:7–8 gives this warning: "Do not deceive yourselves; no one makes a fool of God. A person will reap exactly what he plants. If he plants in the field of his natural desires, from it he will gather the harvest of death; if he plants in the field of the Spirit, he will gather the harvest of eternal life."

Allowing the Past to Control the Present

Whoever suggested that we learn to live "one day at a time" was a very wise person but it is easier said than done for many, especially those who were abused or suffered trauma in the past. The truth of the matter is that no matter what your childhoods may have been like, you now have the choice, as an adult, to move forward and to let go of the past. If you have any unresolved issues from your past, try to work through those issues with supportive Christians, and if necessary, seek professional Christian help.

God doesn't always heal us from everything we may have experienced instantaneously. Ask Him to bring to mind those issues that He wants you to work through in His timing; this may happen every so often over a period of years. Ask Him to heal your memories and to help you forgive anyone if you haven't already. Surrender your past to Him in prayer and ask Him to do with it what He wills, and then let go of it and leave it with Him.

It's a choice to move on to be the person you would like to be, the person you believe God wants you to be. You are no longer bound by your past (2 Corinthians 5:17). Choose to be free of it at this moment. It may be helpful to read the chapter "Overcoming Depression," which has material on how to "reframe" your past.

Then there are others who live in the future: "I will be happy when…" We don't even know if we have tomorrow or the next day. It doesn't exist at this time. I am not saying don't plan and develop goals for yourself, but if you live for the future, you cannot truly appreciate the present. It also reduces anxiety if you know that you only need to be concerned about one day at a time. Matthew 6:34, "So do not worry about tomorrow: it will have enough worries of it's own. There is no need to add to the troubles each day brings."

Purposelessness with no God–Inspired
Goals Resulting in Lethargy

Proverbs 29:18 says, "Where there is no vision, the people perish: but he that keepeth the law, happy is he." Christians need to be seeking God's will regularly to know how He wants to use them for His glory. If you haven't already read Rick Warren's best–selling book *The Purpose Driven Life*, now is the time. It boils down to fulfilling the Great Commission, which is spreading the gospel and to ministry to others.

Every Christian, therefore, needs to know what his gifts/talents/abilities are and where and how and when to use those gifts to fulfill God's purposes in his life. Pray that God will help you to be passionate about the goals He has in mind for you. When you have a sense of how God may want to use you, develop short-and long-term goals to bring this to fruition. So, for example, if you feel you have a ministry to children, you could volunteer to teach Sunday school or take care of little ones in the nursery so that parents may attend church services. If you feel you should be involved in women's ministry, you could develop a Bible study group in your home for women.

If you are not sure what you could be doing, then find a need and fill it. Ask what is needed at your local church or in your community and try out different activities until you have a better sense of what you are gifted for and where God wants you involved in ministry. The chapter "Priorities/Your Purpose in Life" provides a Web site with a spiritual gift inventory to determine your gifts for ministry.

Unconfessed Sin that Makes us Guilty

Numbers 32:23, " And be sure your sin will find you out." When God looks down on us, I believe that He sees us through the veil of the blood of Christ so that He doesn't see our sin. If we have unconfessed sin, however, then our relationship with God is affected which, in turn, affects how He can use us and it will disturb our peace of mind and heart.

Is it important to name our sins? Naming sins is recommended but not commanded. Moses named the sin of his people: idolatry (Exodus 32:31). Ezra, Nehemiah, and Daniel also named specific sins in their prayers (Ezra 9:10–12, 14; Nehemiah 1:7; Daniel 9:5, 6, 10, 11, 14). Sins should be confessed as soon as they are realized to restore your fellowship with God (Psalm 32:5). God's forgiveness is promised for confessing our sins (1 John 1:9).

Failure to confess results in divine discipline (Psalm 32:3–4); however, confession may not remove divine discipline (Joshua 7:19–25; 2 Samuel 12:10–12, 14–23; 24:10–17). If you confess your sins then you are forgiven and if you don't accept God's forgiveness, it is like keeping Jesus nailed to the cross. It is like saying His sacrifice was not good enough to cover your sin, that He suffered and died for nothing. Psalm 139:23–24, "Search me, O God, and know my heart: try me, and know my thoughts: And see if there be any wicked way in me, and lead me in the way everlasting."

Social Isolation and not Being Assertive, Thus Lacking Relationships

Hebrews 10:25 tells us, "Not forsaking the assembling of ourselves together, as the manner of some is; but exhorting one another: and so much the more, as ye see the day approaching." Going to church regularly is very important for a number of reasons: mutual support and encouragement, to grow spiritually, to be used of God according to the abilities He has given you in the body of Christ, for a sense of belonging in the family of God, etc. Not all churches are alike, however, and it is important to find the one God wants you to attend.

Ecclesiastes 4:12 says, "And if one prevail against him, two shall withstand him, and a threefold cord is not quickly broken," and Ecclesiastes 4:9–10 reminds us that "Two are better off than one because together they can work more effectively. If one of them falls down, the other can help him up." God never intended for us to be on our own. No one likes to go to church by himself and many people are a little uncomfortable in new social settings; however, it is vital that we have Christian fellowship and Christian friends in our lives.

If you are not going to church or you have not been to church in some time, check out Alpha Groups; they are non–denominational groups all over the world that provide the opportunity to fellowship with believers and to get established or re–established in your faith (www.alphana.org). If you go to church every week but are still having difficulty connecting with people, then join a cell group or a women's group or single's group or men's group, etc. If necessary, start your own group in your home or at work with other Christians on your lunch hour.

Trying to Control What is out of Our Control Instead of Committing it to God and Trusting Him

It is human nature to want to be in control of as many things as possible in our lives because we perceive such control as security. When we trust God, however, we are acknowledging that He knows best for us and that He won't let us down. The more we try to control, the more we probably thwart God's plan from being fulfilled in our lives.

There is a saying that goes "don't sweat the small stuff, and it's all small stuff." Every circumstance can be divided into the aspects we can control and the aspects we have no control over whatsoever. For example, we cannot control other people, only our reactions to other people. We can plan a vacation in the middle of summer but we still have no control over what the weather will be like while we are on holidays.

We should undertake whatever we can plan for and control, and then the rest? Well, that's where our faith comes in and it is impossible to please God without it (Hebrews 11:6). In Luke 12:25–27 it says, "Can any of you live a bit longer by worrying about it? If you can't manage even such a small thing, why worry about the other things? " Then Jesus goes on to say in verses 30–31,"Your Father knows that you need these things. Instead, be concerned with his Kingdom, and he will provide you with these things."

I like this story of faith found in the book *Shared Grace:* [19]

"When I think of having faith, I always think of the image of the little boy who is in a burning house. The family has escaped, but the father notices that one child, a little boy, has been left behind. The house is blazing and the father cannot go back in to find him. All of a sudden, his son appears at a second story window from which smoke is billowing. He yells, "Jump, son. I will catch you.

The little boy cannot see a thing because of the smoke, so he yells, "But, Dad, I can't see you!" Dad implores: "Jump, son!" The little boy replies again: "But, Dad, I can't see you!" to which the dad says, "But, *I* can see *you*."

That whole image of having faith is like the child jumping out the window when he does not really know for sure his father is going to be there to catch him. Having faith then, is trusting that God is going to be there.

Lack of Biblical Boundaries in Our Lives (emotional, physical, etc.)

According to Cloud and Townsend[20], boundaries help us know what we are/are not responsible for. They keep the good in and bad out, act as an alarm system, help us withdraw, and protect our freedom. There are body boundaries (personal space), words (truth), time, emotional distance, and boundaries in relation to other people. Boundaries give us a sense of purpose, direction, and worth and when violated, we can be depressed, angry, may be unable to finish tasks, and love/receive love appropriately in relationships, etc. Often those who have been abused as children have poor boundaries.

Even Jesus had boundaries, "After healing the invalid, Jesus slipped away" (John 5:13) and, "Early in the morning, he went off to a solitary place to pray" (Mark 1:35). He knew when he needed time for personal reflection and recharging.

Cloud and Townsend have a list of "ten laws of boundaries" in their book. The laws remind us that each individual is responsible for one's own feelings and behaviour, that we cannot change others, and that we need to respect other people's boundaries. We may develop co–dependency if we allow others to determine our identities and what we do.

We need to be able to let others know our personal boundaries by establishing clear limits. For example, if you have a new roommate moving in with you, you need to articulate expectations around lifestyles, housecleaning, and so forth to avoid any misunderstandings. It is okay to say no if we need to regarding anything that would be harmful to us emotionally, physically, or spiritually or if we are overloaded and cannot take on any more projects/tasks. We let people know how to treat us by setting appropriate boundaries of behaviour in our relationships.

Resources:

Boundaries: When to Say Yes, When to Say No—Henry Cloud and John Townsend

Speaking the Truth in Lies– Ruth Koch and Kenneth Haugk

Boundaries Leader's Guide—Sheryl Baar Moon

A Slumbering Spirit (John and Paula Sandford) [54]

To determine if you have a slumbering spirit, ask yourself these questions:

- Do you have difficulty concentrating when reading the Bible and trying to pray?

- Do ever feel the anointing of God over you or through you, or do you just believe in His presence by faith?
- Do you hear the Lord's voice or experience spiritual dreams or visions?
- Do you easily empathize with others during a conversation, or do you need to figure out what you are supposed to say in response with your mind?

If you answer "no" to most of the questions and "yes" to the first question, you may have a slumbering spirit, which is often the result of unforgiveness and judgment toward one or both parents. Pray that the Lord provides the love you did not receive as a child, and after you have forgiven you parents or parent figures, pray that God will woo you into life in your spirit, that your spirit would function with liveliness and enthusiasm from this time forward. Slumbering spirits can be further awakened by the love of others in the body of Christ who continue to encourage them and build them up.

SEVEN STEPS TO SPIRITUAL FREEDOM

The Steps to Freedom in Christ by Neil T. Anderson[21] is something I recommend to every Christian. Each step is different and it is an effective way to unblock any hindrances between you and God, you and others, and will also help you to resolve personal and spiritual conflicts and to break free from bondages.

Step 1—Involvement in Occult–related or Anti–Christian Activities

The first step is basically a checklist of all the activities that you may have, knowingly or unknowingly, gotten involved in before or after becoming a Christian that are actually occult–related or anti–Christian. You see what applies to you and then you pray a prayer of forgiveness and repentance for participating in that activity.

When you accepted Jesus as your Saviour, did you name your sins to God? I am assuming you did initially, not everything comes to mind right away, of course. There are sins of omission and sins of commission. If we had an opportunity to show love or do a kindness and we didn't, that would be a sin of omission. You can pray and ask God to bring to your mind anything that needs to be repented of. It is important that sins are named so we need to pray specifically regarding forgiveness of sins as opposed to, " Lord, forgive me for anything I may have done wrong."

We need to renounce our previous involvement in satanically inspired practices and false religions. You need to renounce any activity and group that denies Jesus Christ or that offers guidance through any source other than the absolute authority of the written Word of God.

Some people are well aware of what activities would be "off limits" for a Christian like séances or playing with Ouija boards and so forth. Unfortunately, a lot of professing Christians seem to think other activities such as playing games like Dungeons and Dragons or having your fortune told or adhering to horoscopes or being hypnotized are okay for them. The truth is that any involvement in occult activity can open doors to the spiritual realm and you are inviting spiritual oppression into your life that may have a significant negative impact on you and your capacity for spiritual growth or victorious Christian living.

Of course, if you were involved in Satanism or witchcraft or channeling or anything of that nature, you may need special prayer and perhaps even deliverance prayer to overcome spiritual oppression. In renouncing these activities, you are declaring that you refuse to follow, obey, or recognize those activities any further in your life.

Any church group, secret society, denomination, organization, or religious order that teaches any gospel other than salvation by grace through faith alone in Jesus Christ as taught in the Bible alone, plus nothing and minus nothing, must be renounced and separated from. All world religions and cults, except biblical Christianity, teach a false gospel (Deuteronomy 18:9–13, Acts 19:18–20).

Step 2—Deception vs. Truth

In Step 2, Anderson covers the ways we can be deceived by the world. Examples are believing that money can buy happiness, that if you are attractive you will get what you want, if you sin you will not be subject to consequences, and so forth. We need to reject any beliefs that are simply contrary to the Word of God.

Ways you deceive yourself are also addressed. For example, hearing God's word but not being obedient to it or thinking you are righteous but you speak in a way that is contrary to the word of God. Anderson also looks at "Ways you Wrongly Defend Yourself." These include: escapism (escaping reality by daydreaming, watching TV or movies, listening to music, playing computer or video games, abusing drugs or alcohol, etc.) and displaced anger (taking out frustrations on innocent people).

A comparative list is offered that examines the lies that we believe about God and His nature in light of the truth, which is the Word of God. For example, the lie that God is insensitive and uncaring is exposed when the Bible says that He is kind and compassionate (Psalm 103:8–14).

Step 3—Unforgiveness

Anderson deals with unforgiveness in Step 3. He cites that forgiveness is not forgetting, that it's a choice and that it is also for our own sake. He suggests listing everyone (or organization) that has ever you hurt you and then praying a prayer of forgiveness. He contends that you will know when you have truly forgiven someone when it is easy to pray for blessings for that person and you have given up the desire to "make them pay" for how they offended or hurt you.

More help with forgiveness is covered in my chapter "Forgiveness is Essential."

Step 4—Rebellion

1 Samuel 15:23, "For rebellion is like the sin of divination (witchcraft) and arrogance (stubbornness) is like the evil of idolatry."

Anderson distinguishes between rebellion and stubbornness: rebellion is disrespect and disobedience to authorities placed over us by God (government, police, teachers, parents, guardians, employers, spouses to each other, church leaders, God's commands). Stubbornness is more about not being teachable. Submission is not required, however, if it is in violation of God's Word. A prayer naming how we have been rebellious or stubborn follows.

I would like to address disrespect toward all parent figures. You will notice in the Ten Commandments, the only commandment with a condition attached to it is "respect your father and your mother, as I, the Lord God command you, so that all may go well with you and so that you may live a long time in the land that I am giving to you" (Deuteronomy 5:11–21, GNB). The implication is there, that perhaps, if we *don't* honour parent figures that it might not go well for us. In other words, it is possible that we could bring negative circumstances into our lives as a consequence for this kind of disobedience to His Word.

You can be sure of one thing, if you dishonoured your parents or parent figures in any way, your children will dishonour you. That means even if you judge your parent in any way, for example, thinking that your mother was a bad mother, that you are dishonouring them. It may well be the case that your father was an alcoholic or your mother was abusive; however, according to God's Word, we are to honour them nonetheless. Even if a parent has passed on, one can ask God for forgiveness for judging them or dishonouring them in any way and we can begin honouring their memory by choosing to believe and remember only positive things about them. And, if your parent figures are still alive, it will be up to you to make sure that you no longer judge or disrespect them in any way if you want God's blessings and you don't want to block your relationship with Him in any way from now on.

Step 5—Pride

Anderson defines pride as "trusting or depending on any source, other than God, to meet our deepest needs for identity, security, safety, and significance" and relying on our own strength, resources, and understanding. Humility, on the other hand, is when we recognize our weaknesses and failures and we seek to find help first by seeking God in prayer and then in His Word.

"Trust in the Lord with all your heart and lean not on your own understanding; in all your ways acknowledge Him, and He will make your paths straight" (Proverbs 3:5–7).

Anderson suggests that "those who are proud and stubborn are opening themselves up to demonic involvement because demons are also proud and stubborn" (1 Peter 5:1–10). Some manifestations of pride are: relying on our own opinions and experience even when it contradicts God's Word, trying to control that which only God can control, and refusing to admit when we are wrong. A prayer to repent of every example of pride in our lives that we can think of ensues.

Step 6—Habitual Sin

Many Christians feel trapped in an endless cycle of sin–confess–sin–confess–sin–confess that continues throughout their lives. Anderson encourages us to "accept that Jesus broke the power of sin over our lives, and by faith we turn away from the sin and toward God." He describes confession as agreement with God that the sins we commit do grieve the Holy Spirit and focuses on the need to repent and accept that Jesus' sacrifice on the Cross broke the power of sin in our lives.

Jesus says, "Go and sin no more. I do not condemn you" (John 8:11). Our responsibility is to go and sin no more and refuse any condemnation so that we don't give up or give in to shame.

We need to name specific sins—everything from adultery, to bitterness, to dependency on others, to despair, discontent with God's will, excessive self–pity, fear of man, impatience, lust, striving, vanity, worry—the list can be quite exhaustive. It is essential, however, for Christians to be able to recognize the areas within themselves and in their lives that need freedom. Every sin will rob us of joy, peace, hope, and other blessings that can be ours and that God wishes for us. Name those sins in prayer and repent of them.

Step 7—Generational Curses

The concept of generational curses and blessings is a biblical one; however, we can replace curses with the truth and be set free from them. Common generational curses are family violence, poverty, pre–marital pregnancy, addictive behaviours, divorce, mental illness, and immorality.

The prayer that follows is a declaration that you will now reject and disown all the sins and iniquities of your ancestors (naming all you can think of) based on the fact that we have been delivered from the power of darkness and translated into the Kingdom of God's dear Son (Colossians 1:1–3). The prayer also renounces and cancels any satanic assignments that may have been directed to you or on your ministry in the name of Jesus. We are committed to the Lord Jesus Christ and by His authority, we commit ourselves to do God's will.

Anderson warns his readers that once completing the seven steps, they may experience some spiritual opposition. He admonishes us to maintain our freedom by continuing a right relationship with God and by choosing to believe the Word of God and standing firm in the power of our Lord Jesus Christ. To maintain a right relationship with God, ensure that you are renewing your mind in the Word and that you are being obedient to God's commands (refer to Part One chapters of Basic Training).

For your encouragement and further study, read *Victory Over Darkness* (youth version: *Stomping Out the Darkness*), *The Bondage Breaker*, and *Released from Bondage*. If you are a parent, read *Spiritual Protection for Your Children*.

Resources:

Freedom in Christ Ministries—www.ficm.org

Ministering the Steps to Freedom in Christ—
Neil Anderson

Helping Others Find Freedom in Christ (training manual and study guide also available) Neil Anderson

Bondage Breaker—Neil Anderson—
ISBN # 0–7369–0241–4

Victory over Darkness—Neil Anderson—
ISBN # 0–8307–2564–4

The Steps to Freedom in Christ workbook—
Neil Anderson—ISBN # 0–8307–1850–8

SPIRITUAL OPPOSITION

"When the enemy shall come in like a flood, the Spirit of the Lord shall lift up a standard against him" (Isaiah 59:19).

The Bible teaches us that evil spirits exist just as God's angels do. "For our struggle is not against flesh and blood, but against the rulers, against the authorities against the powers of this dark world and against the spiritual forces of evil in the heavenly realms" (Ephesians 6:12, NIV). Of course we need a balance here. As Christians we can't go around attributing everything negative in our lives to demons; however, they are real and active and Christians do have to contend with spiritual opposition in their lives at times.

Christians can be oppressed by demons or bound spiritually in different ways. Thankfully, 1 John 4:4 reminds us that, "Ye are of God, little children, and have overcome them: because greater is he that is in you (the Holy Spirit of God) than he that is in the world (the devil)."

If you know someone who is being influenced by evil spirits, you need to proceed with the utmost caution and consult with a pastor or professional or someone who has a proven deliverance ministry with the gift of discernment.

Renunciation of the Occult

Hal Weeks[22] offers the following information on spiritual cleansing.

> Any involvement in the occult is an abomination to God. Even a trivial interest in these areas can have severe and prolonged consequences. It is important to understand that you can renounce occult involvement for yourself and also for your ancestors who may have been involved in any of these practices. Such involvement can affect descendants to the third and fourth generation.

> "The Lord is slow to anger, abounding in love and forgiving sin and rebellion. Yet he does not leave the guilty unpunished; he punishes the children for the sin of the fathers to the third and fourth generation" (Numbers 14:18, NIV).

> There shall not be found among you anyone who makes his son or his daughter pass through the fire, one who uses divination, one who practices witchcraft, or one who interprets omens, or a sorcerer, or one who casts a spell, or a medium, or a spiritist, or one who calls up the dead. For whoever does these things is detestable to the Lord; and because of these detestable things the Lord your God will drive them out before you. Deuteronomy 18:10–12 (NIV)

Although there is much to be said about this subject, making the following confession has proven to be effective:

> "Dear Lord, I have a confession to make. Through ignorance, or wilfulness, I have sought supernatural experiences apart from You. I have disobeyed your Word and I ask you to deliver me, as I renounce all these things. Cleanse me in body, mind, soul, and spirit, I pray, in Jesus' name.

I, for myself and my ancestors, renounce, forsake, and turn away from all contact with witchcraft, magic, Ouija boards, and other occult games.

I renounce, for myself and my ancestors, all kinds of fortune telling, palm reading, tea leaves reading, crystal balls, tarot, and other card laying.

I renounce, for myself and my ancestors, all astrology, birth signs, and horoscopes.

I renounce, for myself and my ancestors, the heresy of reincarnation and all healing groups involved in metaphysics and spiritualism.

I renounce, for myself and my ancestors, all hypnosis under any excuse or authority.

I renounce, for myself and my ancestors, all music that in any way is contrary to the Word of God.

I renounce, for myself and my ancestors, all transcendental meditation and all other Eastern cults and idol worship.

I renounce, for myself and my ancestors, all martial arts, including judo, kung fu, and karate that in any way convey supernatural power that is not from God.

I renounce, for myself and my ancestors, all water witching (or dowsing), levitation, table–tipping, psychometry (divination through objects), automatic writing, and handwriting analysis.

I renounce, for myself and my ancestors, all literature I have ever read and studies in any of these fields. I promise I will destroy all such material in my possession.

I renounce, for myself and my ancestors, astral projection, soul, and out–of–body travel and other demonic skills.

I renounce, for myself and my ancestors, in the name of the Lord Jesus Christ, all psychic power that I may have inherited and break any demonic hold or curse on my family line back to ten or more generations on both sides of the family.

I renounce, for myself and my ancestors, and forsake every psychic and occult contact that I am unaware of, as well as those I may have forgotten.

I renounce, for myself and my ancestors, every cult that denies atonement through the blood of Jesus Christ and every philosophy that denies His deity.

I promise to destroy any occult paraphernalia that I posses since they are an abomination. Now, Satan, I cast down any strongholds that these activities may have established, and close any door I may have opened to you through these contacts, in the name of Jesus Christ."

Get rid of anything of an occult nature, such a Ouija boards, tarot cards, good luck charms, fetishes, Tiki dolls, idols, rabbit's feet, horseshoes, charm bracelets, astrology items, and frog or owl items. It is a good practice to ask the Holy Spirit to reveal to you anything He would want you to get rid of. Obviously, you would not want to give them to someone else. They may have cost you something to acquire them, but it will not cost you anything to get rid of them.

Powerful Personal Prayer by Victor Matthews[23]

"Heavenly Father, I bow in worship and praise before you. I cover myself with the blood of the Lord Jesus Christ as my protection. I surrender myself completely and unreservedly in every area of my life to You. I take a stand against all the workings of Satan that would hinder me in my prayer life. I address myself only to the True and Living God and refuse any involvement of Satan in my prayer. Satan, I command you, in the name of the Lord Jesus Christ, to leave my presence with all your demons. I bring the blood of the Lord Jesus Christ between us. It surrounds me like a mighty wall that you cannot penetrate. Heavenly Father, I worship You and give You praise. Heavenly Father, I recognize that You are worthy to receive all glory and honour and praise. I renew my allegiance to you. I am thankful that the victory the Lord Jesus Christ won for me on the Cross and in His resurrection has been given to me and that I am seated with the Lord Jesus Christ in the heavenlies. I take my place with Him in the heavenlies and recognize by faith that all wicked spirits and Satan himself are under my feet. I declare, therefore, that Satan and his wicked spirits are subject to me in the name of the Lord Jesus Christ. I am thankful for the armour You have provided. I put on the Girdle of Truth, the Breastplate of Righteousness, the Sandals of Peace, and the Helmet of Salvation. I lift up the Shield of Faith against all the fiery darts of the enemy, and I take in my hand the Sword of the Spirit, the Word of God. I choose to use Your Word against all the forces of evil in my life.

I reject all the insinuations and accusations and the temptations of Satan. I affirm that the Word of God is true and I choose to live today in the light of God's Word. I choose, Heavenly Father, to live in obedience to You and in fellowship with Yourself.

Open my eyes and show me the areas of my life that do not please You. Work in me to cleanse me from all ground that would give Satan a foothold against me. I do in every way stand into all that it means to be Your adopted child and I welcome all the ministry of the Holy Spirit. By faith and in dependence upon You, I put off the fleshly works of the evil one and stand into all the victory of the crucifixion where the Lord Jesus Christ provided cleansing from the old nature. I put on Your holiness and stand into all the victory of the resurrection and the provision He has made for me to live above sin. Therefore, today I put off all forms of selfishness and put on the new nature with its love.

I recognize that this is Your will for me and I therefore reject and resist all the endeavours of Satan and his wicked spirits to rob me of the will of God. I refuse in this day to believe my feelings and I hold up the Shield of Faith against all the accusations and distortion and insinuations that Satan would put into my mind. I claim the fullness of the will of God for my life today. In the name of the Lord Jesus Christ, I completely surrender myself to You, Heavenly Father, as a living sacrifice. I choose not to be conformed to this world. I choose to be transformed by the renewing of my mind, and I pray that You would show me Your will and enable me to walk in all the fullness of Your will today.

I am thankful, Heavenly Father, that the weapons of our warfare are not carnal but mighty through God from the pulling down of strongholds, to the casting down of imagination and every high thing that exalteth itself against the knowledge of God, and to bring every thought into obedience to the Lord Jesus Christ. Therefore, in my own life today I tear down the strongholds of Satan and smash the plans of Satan that have been formed against me. I tear down the strongholds of Satan against my mind, and I surrender my mind to You, blessed Holy Spirit.

I rejoice in Your mercy and goodness, Heavenly Father. I pray that now and through this day You would strengthen and enlighten me. Show me the way Satan is hindering and tempting and lying and distorting the truth in my life. I cover myself with the blood of the Lord Jesus Christ and pray that You, blessed Holy Spirit, would bring all the work of the crucifixion, all the work of the resurrection, all the work of the glorification, and all the work of Pentecost into my life today. I surrender myself to You. I refuse to be discouraged. You are the God of all hope. You have proven your power by resurrecting Jesus Christ from the dead, and I claim in every way this victory over all the satanic forces in my life. I pray in the name of the Lord Jesus Christ with thanksgiving and praise to You alone. Amen."

"Behold, I give to you power to tread on serpents and scorpions, and over all the power of the enemy: and nothing shall by any means hurt you" (Luke 10:19).

Resources:

http://www.wholeperson–counseling.org/door/open.html This is a great page that explains how we can be oppressed by evil spirits and how to be set free.

http://www.doveministries.com/usa/pamphlets/counsellingpray. htm Bill Subritzky's Web site has a checklist of occult activities; make sure you have not knowingly or unknowingly participated in any listed. He also has a prayer of deliverance on that page as well as a prayer to renounce inner vows, soul ties, release from curses, prayer for healing, and a prayer for masons.

His free articles include dealing with fear and keys to healing and deliverance.

http://www.sw–mins.org/Deliverance_ministries.htm
Deliverance ministries in North America

Recommended Reading

The Bondage Breaker and *Steps to Freedom in Christ* by Neil Anderson

Deliverance From Evil Spirits, by Frances McNutt covers: clearing away misconceptions about deliverance, the scriptural basis for deliverance, curses and the power of false judgment, preparation for deliverance ministry, praying for deliverance, and the deliverance of places.

They Shall Expel Demons by Derek Prince. Prince offers practical advice on how to receive and minister deliverance and how to remain free. He also describes nine characteristic activities of demons, seven ways demons gain access to people's lives, and then leads you through nine steps to deliverance.

Part Three:

HELP FOR SPECIFIC ISSUES

These things I have spoken unto you, that in me ye might have peace. In the world ye shall have tribulation: but be of good cheer; I have overcome the world.

John 16:33

2 Kings 20:5 "I have seen your tears, I will heal you."

ACCEPTING GOD'S LOVE

Most Christians have a head knowledge that God loves them but many Christians have difficulty in truly receiving and accepting God's love for them in a real, personal way. This is understand-able since you cannot see God and our interaction with Him is limited and often appears one-sided. When people love us, they demonstrate it in various ways, which affirms their love for us; however, with God, we have to choose to believe that He's lov-ing and that He loves us even when we don't "feel" it.

We know He loved us enough to send His own son to die for us but how much does He really love you or me? I asked Him once and He told me He loved me "oceansful." I knew it was the Lord speaking to my heart and mind because I never would have thought of that response on my own. I kept trying to imagine how big an ocean was and then how vast more than one ocean could be. I tried to grasp the concept of "oceans of love" and frankly, I still can't comprehend that one but I know it's an awful lot of deep love and concern and God feels that much love for each and every one of us.

It might help if you do a Bible study where you look up all the verses in the Bible that mention God loving us or His caring nature such as "God is love" (1 John 4:8, 1 John 4:16). He *is* love, His nature is love, He *feels* love toward each of us. Go to www.fathersloveletter.com to see a wonderful video on how much God loves you. Here are the words in text:

My Child[24]...

You may not know me, but I know everything about you...

Psalm 139:1

I know when you sit down and when you rise up...

Psalm 139:2

I am familiar with all your ways...

Psalm 139:3

Even the very hairs on your head are numbered...

Matthew 10:29–31

For you were made in my image...

Genesis 1:27

In me you live and move and have your being...

Acts 17:28

For you are my offspring...

Acts 17:28

I knew you even before you were conceived...

Jeremiah 1:4–5

I chose you when I planned creation...

Ephesians 1:11–12

You were not a mistake, for all your days are written in my book...

Psalm 139:15–16

I determined the exact time of your birth and where you would live…

Acts 17:26

You are fearfully and wonderfully made…

Psalm 139:14

I knit you together in your mother's womb…

Psalm 139:13

And brought you forth on the day you were born…

Psalm 71:6

I have been misrepresented by those who don't know me…

John 8:41–44

I am not distant and angry, but am the complete expression of love…

1 John 4:16

And it is my desire to lavish my love on you…

1 John 3:1

Simply because you are my child and I am your father…

1 John 3:1

I offer you more than your earthly father ever could…

Matthew 7:11

For I am the perfect father…

Matthew 5:48

Every good gift that you receive comes from my hand…

James 1:17

For I am your provider and I meet all your needs…

Matthew 6:31–33

My plan for your future has always been filled with hope…

Jeremiah 29:11

Because I love you with an everlasting love…

Jeremiah 31:3

My thoughts toward you are countless as the sand on the seashore…

Psalm 139:17–18

And I rejoice over you with singing…

Zephaniah 3:17

I will never stop doing good to you…

Jeremiah 32:40

For you are my treasured possession…

Exodus 19:5

I desire to establish you with all my heart and all my soul…

Jeremiah 32:41

If you seek me with all your heart, you will find me…

Deuteronomy 4:29

Delight in me and I will give you the desires of your heart…

Psalm 37:4

For it is I who gave you those desires…

Philippians 2:13

I am able to do more for you than you could possibly imagine…

Ephesians 3:20

For I am your greatest encourager…

2 Thessalonians 2:16–17

I am also the Father who comforts you in all your troubles…

2 Corinthians 1:3–4

When you are brokenhearted, I am close to you…

Psalm 34:18

As a shepherd carries a lamb, I have carried you close to my heart…

Isaiah 40:11

One day I will wipe away every tear from your eyes…

Revelation 21:3–4

And I'll take away all the pain you have suffered on this earth…

Revelation 21:3–4

I am your Father, and I love you even as I love my son, Jesus…

John 17:23

For in Jesus, my love for you is revealed…

John 17:26

He is the exact representation of my being…

Hebrews 1:3

He came to demonstrate that I am for you, not against you…

Romans 8:31

And to tell you that I am not counting your sins…

2 Corinthians 5:18–19

Jesus died so that you and I could be reconciled…

2 Corinthians 5:18–19

His death was the ultimate expression of my love for you…

1 John 4:10

I gave up everything I loved that I might gain your love…

Romans 8:31–32

If you receive the gift of my son Jesus, you receive me…

1 John 2:23

And nothing will ever separate you from my love again…

Romans 8:38–39

Come home and I'll throw the biggest party heaven has ever seen…

Luke 15:7

I have always been Father, and will always be Father…

Ephesians 3:14–15

My question is…Will you be my child?…

John 1:12–13

Although God is referred to as the "Father" in the Bible with parental attributes, did you know that God has maternal attributes as well? In Isaiah 66:13, God says, "As one whom his mother comforteth, so will I comfort you; and ye shall be comforted in Jerusalem." In Matthew 23:37 Jesus tells us how he wished he could gather the people of Jerusalem to himself as a mother hen gathers her chicks under her wings. Jesus welcoming the little children is another loving image.

Part of the problem in perceiving God as a loving parent can be that we often compare God "our Father" with our earthly parents. This is especially difficult if our earthly parents were abusive. Let's compare how different God is than earthly parents:[25]

Earthly Parents:

– can be abusive

– can be unloving
  and cruel

– may punish in anger

– may not have the child's
  best interests

– wrong motivation

– impatient

– may neglect or abandon
  their own children

– may be unpredictable

– may not be concerned with
  our well–being

– may be unforgiving

God as Parent:

– is never abusive

– always loves
  unconditionally

– teaches in love

– always has our best
  interest at heart

– always motivated by
  love toward us

– always patient and
  understanding

– will never leave us or
  abandon us

– can always be counted
  on as loving

– always concerned with
  our well–being

– always forgiving

– add any others you can think of

Seeing God Differently

"God is represented in Jesus, and everything Jesus does is a reflection of God. God had to become human to communicate who God is and what God is like. What then, does the Bible teach us about Jesus? We never find Jesus abusing people in the Bible, quite the contrary. In the book of Luke, Jesus is depicted as reaching out to the poor, the outcasts, the wounded. To these people, his response is mercy and compassion."[26]

And that is how Jesus sees you, with mercy, compassion, and unfailing love. He is the shepherd of the sheep, gently guiding them, bringing back the strays with love, protecting them constantly, watching over them continuously, keeping them safe, taking care of them, meeting all their needs. He cares for you even more tenderly.

Neil T. Anderson[27] makes a list of negative beliefs we may need to repent of:

I renounce the lie that my Father God is…	I declare the truth that my Father God is…
1. Distant and uninterested.	Intimate and involved. (Psalm 139: 1–18)
2. Insensitive and uncaring.	Kind and compassionate. (Psalm 103:8–14)
3. Stern and demanding.	Accepting and filled with joy and love. (Zephaniah 3:17, Romans 15:7)

I renounce the lie that my Father God is…	I declare the truth that my Father God is…
4. Passive and cold.	Warm and affectionate. (Isaiah 40:11, Hosea 11:3,4)
5. Absent or too busy for me.	Always with me and eager to be with me. (Jeremiah 31:20, Ezekiel 34:11–16, Hebrews 13:5)
6. Never satisfied with what I do, impatient, or angry.	Patient and slow to anger. (Exodus 34:6, II Peter 3:9)
7. Mean, cruel, or abusive.	Loving, gentle, and protective of me. (Psalm 18:2, Jeremiah 31:13, Isaiah 42:3)
8. Trying to take all the fun out of life.	Trustworthy and wants to give me a full life: His will is good, perfect, and acceptable. (Lamentations 3:22,23 John 10:10, Romans 12:1,2)
9. Controlling or manipulative.	Full of grace and mercy: He gives me freedom to fail. (Luke 15: 11–16: Hebrews 4:15,16)

I renounce the lie that my Father God is...	I declare the truth that my Father God is...
10. Condemning or unforgiving.	Tenderhearted and forgiving: His heart and arms are always open to me. (Psalms 130:1–4, Luke 15:17–24)
11. Nit–picking, exacting, or perfectionistic.	Committed to my growth and proud of me as His growing child. (Romans 8:28, 29, II Corinthians 7:4; Hebrews 12:5–11)

Lord, I confess that I have chosen to believe these lies about You (name all that apply)_____. Thank you for your forgiveness. I now commit myself to right attitudes toward your character. In Jesus' name, amen.

Once you truly grasp how loving and patient God is toward you and you are able to accept and receive His love, then you are set free from trying to please others or trying to win other people's love. No one will ever know you completely or love you completely like He does. There is nothing you can do or not do to make Him love you any less than He does at this moment. His love for you will not go away or dwindle over time. You will always be the apple of His eye, but it is up to you to choose to believe that.

Jesus Is with You by Roy Lessin[28]

You never need to think of yourself as forsaken,
because Jesus has called you His own.
You never need to think of yourself as alone,
because Jesus is with you always.
You never need to think of yourself as rejected,
because Jesus holds you in His arms.
You never need to think of yourself as defenseless,
because Jesus is your protector.

You never need to think of yourself as inadequate,
because Jesus is your provider.
You never need to think of yourself as useless,
because Jesus has a purpose and plan for your life.
You never need to think of yourself as hopeless,
because Jesus is your future.
You never need to think of yourself as defeated,
because Jesus is your victory.

You never need to think of yourself as weak,
because Jesus is your strength.
You never need to think of yourself as perplexed,
because Jesus is your peace.
You never need to think of yourself as needy,
because Jesus is your daily provider.
You never need to think of yourself as unappreciated,
because Jesus is your everlasting reward.

ANGER MANAGEMENT

Everyone knows the story of Jesus being upset with the money changers in the temple (John 2:14–15). Ephesians 4:26 warns us to, "Be ye angry, and sin not: let not the sun go down upon your wrath." The sin, then, is not in being angry but in expressing the anger in unhealthy ways that may pose a risk of harm to oneself or another person or in holding a grudge and not letting go of the anger. It is important to understand what thoughts and feelings are at the root of the anger. Often it is a feeling of being hurt or feeling inadequate or feeling you have been wronged. Once you have identified the underlying feelings, you can address them directly.

You probably need professional help for anger management if your anger is controlling your behaviour instead of you controlling your emotions. If you have ever hit somebody, broken things, or punched walls then you could benefit from an anger management course. If you lose your temper daily and feel frustrated when trying to express yourself, then you need to find healthy ways to communicate, which will also improve your relationships.

It is vital to understand that you are in control of your emotions and your emotions are not in control of you. Anyone who says that they just have a bad temper or that it is "just the way they are" is simply stating that they don't want to change or they see no need to change. As Christians, however, we need to be able to control our emotions, especially anger. It is also a fallacy to think or say that someone "made you angry." We choose how we react to people. It is totally possible, even in the worst situations, to calm yourself immediately and talk yourself out of a negative response.

The following is an exercise by Leonard Ingram, PhD[29], to measure your anger and to identify the roots of it.

Measure Your Anger

1. How am I feeling right now?

___ Anxious ___ Worthless ___ Hostile ___ Depressed ___ Mean/evil ___ Revengeful ___ Bitter ___ Rebellious ___ Paranoid ___ Victimized ___ Numb ___ Sarcastic ___ Resentful ___ Frustrated ___ Destructive ___ Irritable

These are some of the names that we give to our feelings of anger! There is no cure for any of them. The first step in resolving our anger problem is to identify it as anger! The purpose of this step is to make our anger more specific. No one can manage anger that is vague and covered up with euphemisms.

2. What happened to make you angry?

If we can focus on the specific incident that triggered our anger, our anger becomes more understandable and easier to manage.

_____

_____

_____

_____

_____

3. Who am I angry at?

___ My own self ___ My spouse ___ My partner ___ My boss
___ The kids ___ God ___ The Human Race ___ My Life ___
All men ___ Women ___ Other races ___ Miscellaneous

Our anger usually will involve five general areas.

1) Our anger at others, (2) Others' anger at us, (3) Our anger at self, (4) Residual anger from the past, or (5) Abstract anger.

Now that you have established the fact that you are angry and that your anger has an "object" in the real world, you are ready for the fourth step in working through the anger process. You are ready to factor your anger into its main components. If you can identify the specific facets of your anger, you will be in a better position to put your anger into a more moderate and more manageable perspective. You can do this by asking yourself a series of focusing questions.

4. How did the situation make me feel besides angry?

(Example #1: I resent being forced to give into them all the time. It makes me feel powerless!)

(Example #2: His criticisms of me make me feel unappreciated and good for nothing.)

_____

_____

_____

_____

_____

Now that you have pin-pointed your feelings underlying your anger, you are now ready to put your anger in a clearer perspective. The next step is to "peel" your anger down to the next layer.

5. What about this angers me the most?

For example, you have established the fact that in the above situation it made you feel powerless, unappreciated, or good for nothing. You are now ready to take a closer look at these feelings underlying your anger. What is it about being made to feel powerless that angers you the most? Some examples of what you might find upon deeper analysis are:

– "There is nothing that I can do about it."

– "I feel so stupid!"

– "I feel guilty for allowing it to happen."

– "I feel inadequate to cope with this situation."

Having peeled your anger down to this level, you are ready now to penetrate your anger at its deepest level. You are ready to focus on the real issue underlying all of the prior layers and levels of your emotional distress.

6. Now, what about this angers me the *most*?

This level of self–analysis usually brings us down to bedrock. Down to the fundamental issue that underlies all the others and that must be identified and relieved if we are to strengthen our vulnerability to mismanaging our anger, and making our lives more miserable than it needs to be. The answer found at this level of self–analysis often turns out to be, "I feel so worthless!" It is hard for us to respect someone who is stupid, helpless, inadequate, and powerless! And when we have those feelings toward ourselves, they destroy our respect for ourselves.

We lose our self–respect and hold ourselves in contempt. The final step in managing our anger consists of replacing these feeling or worthlessness—even unworthy of our *own* respect—with its specific antidote. The only antidote for self–contempt is self–respect.

Four Proven Techniques for Managing Anger[30]

The first step toward managing anger in our personal relationships appropriately is the identification of the mistaken attitudes and convictions that predispose us to being excessively angry in the first place! Once these mistakes have been corrected, we will be less likely to fly off the handle than we were in the past.

The second step is the identification of those factors from our childhood that prevent us from expressing our anger as appropriately as we otherwise might. These factors include fear, denial, ignorance, and so on.

These impediments to the effective and appropriate management of our anger toward others can be removed so that our suppressed anger will *not* compound itself inside of us as it has been doing for years.

The third step is learning the appropriate modes of expressing our "legitimate" anger at others so that we can begin to cope more effectively with anger–provoking situations as they arise in our personal relationships. When we are anxious or depressed in our relationships, we are often experiencing the consequences of our suppressed anger. The problem is that we have suppressed our anger so deeply that we succeeded in concealing it from our own selves! All we are left with is the residual evidence of it, our anxiety or our depression. When we are depressed, very often we are also angry at our self without realizing it.

Learning to appropriately manage our anger at ourselves is the antidote to much of alcoholism and drug abuse. But the management of our anger does not end in learning these new and more appropriate ways to express it. There remains one last step.

The fourth step in the anger management process is to bind up the wounds that may have been left by the potentially devastating emotional impact of anger—"anger wounds" left in us against those who have wronged us. If we do not complete this mopping up step, we will cling to the resentment of having been done wrong and will carry the festering residue of our anger and rage in our hearts forever.

One of the most effective means of giving ourselves immediate relief from anger in our personal relationships is to forgive others. Many of us cannot forgive those who have trespassed against us.

Something below the level of our conscious awareness prevents us from relieving our residual anger by forgiving the other person and we then carry a grudge in our hearts for thirty years! This unresolved anger poisons our relationship with our friends and loved ones. It even spoils our relationship with ourselves! We make our own lives mean and miserable instead of happy and full. Very often the feeling is, *Why should I forgive them? What they did was wrong!* But, is forgiveness for those who only do us right? Most people have a hard time forgiving others simply because they have a wrong understanding of what for-giveness is! When you forgive someone, it does not mean that you condone or are legitimizing their behaviour toward you. To forgive them means that you refuse to carry painful and debili-tating grudges around with you for the rest of your life! You are "refusing" to cling to the resentment of them having done you wrong. You are giving yourself some immediate relief from your *own* anger!

To forgive, then, is an act that we do on our *own* behalf. It has nothing to do with "lifting" the other person's sin! You are not doing it for their sake. You are doing it for yourself. This is a choice you are making on your *own* terms in order to relieve your *own* pent–up emotions.

Time–Out

If you feel yourself getting angry, take a "cooling down" period to think things over and calm down. If in a heated discussion with someone else, let them know that you want to continue the conversation and work things out but that you just need some time to regroup first. Leave that area if possible for at least twenty minutes or until you feel you have gained self–control.

Take slow, deep breaths—you can even say that with every inhaling breath you are taking in peace, joy, and love and with every exhaling breath you are releasing tension, anger, and resentment. This will help in slowing your heart rate and in lowering your blood pressure.

During your time–out, practice positive self–talk with statements that you say to yourself such as:

- I have nothing to prove right now.

- I am going to stay calm so that I am in control of my emotions.

- I choose how I react to other people and I refuse to let anger get the best of me.

- I accept myself regardless of what others think of me and I have God's approval.

- God is with me. I do not need to feel threatened.

- I know that I cannot control other people and certain situations, but I can control myself and I choose to express my feelings and thoughts in a healthy fashion.

- I am human. It's okay to make mistakes. If people criticize me, I will survive.

- I don't need to respond in anger to someone else's anger. If I stay calm, they will calm down as well. If they don't, I will take a time–out so we can both cool down.

- Most things are not worth arguing about. My reactions may be triggering emotions from similar situations in the past. I have been hurt or feel scared, but can handle this now.

Galatians 5:25–26 reminds us, "If we live in the Spirit, let us also walk in the Spirit. Let us not be desirous of vain glory, provoking one another, envying one another."

If you have done a time–out but you find yourself getting angry again when returning to the situation/person, try a different approach, repeat the time–out or take a longer time–out.

Points to Remember

1. You are responsible for and in control of your reactions and responses. No one else can "make you angry."

2. The sooner we accept unfair situations, the sooner we can strengthen our faith and move forward.

3. Most things are not in your control so let go and let God handle those things.

4. Angry people make others uncomfortable.

5. Vent your feelings to God in prayer or to a good friend or write it out in a journal. Find something that relaxes you: worship music, exercise, drawing, reading the Word, etc. and do it on a regular basis.

How to Express Your Feelings

If you have a problem with someone, let them know what you are feeling. Before you do that, however, think through what you will say and how you will deal with possible responses. Pray about it—is this something you should let pass and deal with on your own? Have you processed what is at the root of your anger reaction and dealt with the source of it? Is it something you can work through on your own?

If you have decided you need to talk to the other person, try these rules as a guideline for how to handle the conversation:

Dos:

- Be specific about what you are upset about exactly. Use the formula:

- When you _____ then I feel _____ because _____.

- Speak calmly. State your feelings using "I" statements to articulate how you feel about the situation, not about the person.

- Request a small change. Request only one or two changes at one time and tell them what specific behaviours you want to see stopped or increased.

- State how their change in behaviour will help you, them, and/or your relationship with them.

- Validate the other person's thoughts and feelings.

- Allow yourself to be vulnerable.

Don'ts:

- Don't use vague terms or generalize.

- Don't assume you know the other person's intentions or motives.

- Don't allow yourself to have an emotional outburst.

- Don't put the other person down or attack their character.

- Don't request too big of a change or ask for too many changes at once.

- Don't assume that you don't have anything to work on to improve the situation.

- Don't threaten or try to bully or control the other person.

Resources:

If you go to http://members.tripod.com/kanchand/anger.htm you will find some important facts about anger and there is also an anger test you can take on that page.

The book *Managing and Coping With Anger* by Leonard Ingram contains an in–depth analysis of this four–step process plus ten carefully designed exercises to help you to completely master the anger management process. www.angermgmt.com The same site offers an anger management toolkit at http://www.angermgmt.com/angertoolkit.asp that will help you to deal with the underlying roots of your anger.

DATING/SEXUALITY

Dating is supposed to be the process of selecting potential life partners. Teenagers may not have matured enough emotionally and/or spiritually to be considering marriage. It would be wiser for teenagers to maintain platonic friendships with members of the opposite sex or if they do "date" to do it on with a group of friends that they know well, as opposed to one–on–one dates.

I think everyone knows that a Christian should only date another Christian (2 Corinthians 6:14). Even then, people can be on different spiritual levels or they may disagree on different doctrinal issues. You should consider compatibility with someone in all areas: physical (in terms of physical attraction), emotional, spiritual, intellectual, social, etc. If you are dating someone, pay attention to any "red flags" you may notice about them such as: addictions, emotional immaturity (irresponsibility), anger management problems, a lack of a spiritual commitment, and so forth.

Hopefully, I do not even have to point out to anyone that pre–marital sex is against God's commands. 1 Corinthians 6:18 simply states, "Flee fornication. Every sin that a man doeth is without the body, but he that committeth fornication sinneth against his own body." It is a bit of an unusual way of looking at it, but I tell single people that if they have pre–marital sex, that is like cheating on their future spouse in a way. When two people engage in sex, they create a bond, more than just a physical bond, that should only exist if they are married to each other.

If you have had sex with someone that you are not married to, you need to ask God to forgive you for having sex with that person—name them in the prayer and ask God to break any ties you have with that person in Jesus' name.

The easiest way to ensure that you are able to overcome sexual temptation when dating is to make a rule that the two of you will not allow yourselves to be alone in a private place together. If you are always in a public place or if there is always an accountable person in the home, then you are much less likely to find yourselves in tempting situations.

If you are engaged, it is important to discuss topics such as: money, disciplining kids, housework, issues of trust, abuse, and communication. Attend a pre-marital course or meet with your pastor to discuss these issues. Make sure you can resolve conflicts in a way that works for both of you before you get married. You cannot be in a right relationship with God if you are engaging in pre-marital sex or if you are married and engaging in sexual activity with someone other than your spouse (including pornography). It is not that God is trying to deny anyone pleasure in this life, He is actually trying to protect us from having our hearts broken due to unplanned pregnancies, sexual diseases, and disappointment when relationships end.

Now for the "M" word. I have heard different teaching on the practice of masturbation. I don't think anyone should condemn themselves or feel that they cannot overcome this habit; however, I personally believe that one should attempt to live their Christian life without engaging in masturbation. While the Bible does not mention masturbation specifically, there are plenty of verses related to sexual immorality and lust and many other verses that speak of walking after the Spirit and not after the flesh (Romans 8:4).

One of the fruit of the Spirit that God desires for us is self–control; however, masturbation is often combined with pornography and/or sexual fantasy. "But I say unto you, that whosoever looketh on a woman to lust after her hath committed adultery with her already in his heart" (Matthew 5:28). Masturbation can become an addiction and then Christians find themselves controlled by the flesh and not by the Spirit.

As for the topic of homosexuality, I do not personally believe that anyone is born "gay." I think there are a number of reasons why people end up being attracted to members of the same sex and enter into a gay lifestyle, but I also believe that God can help you to overcome same–sex attraction. There are numerous Christian organizations that help people overcome these temptations.

It is important to remember, though, that as Christians, we are to love the sinner and hate the sin. People struggling with same–sex attraction should always be welcomed and embraced in our churches as long as they are in the process of attempting to overcome any sinful activity in their lives.

The same with anyone committing any other sexual sin, such as adultery or premarital sex, as long as they admit it is contrary to God's Word and they want help to stop sinful behaviour, then they should receive all the support the church community can provide for them.

Married people should not engage in close friendships with members of the opposite sex. I have to admire Billy Graham; I heard he made a vow to himself that he would never be alone in a room with another woman other than his wife to ensure that anything improper could never even begin to develop between him and another woman. What a role model for Christian men!

Tips for Remaining Sexually Pure[31]

1. Develop your own personal boundaries for sexual activity.

2. Make a choice to realign your peer group to include like-minded students who are committed to honoring God and their own personal boundaries in their character and conduct.

3. Find an accountability partner with whom you can be completely open, honest, and vulnerable who can help keep you from falling into temptation that could lead to sexual activity.

4. Share your pledge of sexual purity with significant relationships (parents, dates, close friends) to help underscore the seriousness of your commitment.

5. Make careful decisions about whom to date and where dating activity takes place.

6. If you make a bad choice, promptly admit it and get back on track.

7. Remind yourself often that premarital sexual activity can result in unwanted pregnancies, sexually transmitted dis-

ease, emotional problems, and spiritual problems, to name a few of the consequences.

8. Walk away, use the telephone, or call a parent or friend if you find yourself in a compromising situation.

9. Be of help to a friend in his or her fight to remain sexually pure.

10. Avoid all drugs and situations where they are likely to be present.

11. Avoid all drinking situations or occasions.

12. Don't let yourself become overly dependent on another person.

13. Seek knowledgeable help when you feel weak.

14. Live in *today*, not yesterday.

15. When in doubt, ask questions. The only stupid question is the one not asked.

16. Be willing to go to any lengths to stay sexually pure.

17. Be honest and consistent. These behaviors are fundamental to maintaining sexual purity.

If you are married and had an affair or you think you might have developed a close bond with someone that you shouldn't have, it might be helpful for you to say the following prayer.

Training–Wheel Prayer for Breaking
Soul Ties by Liberty Savard[32]

"Lord, I have been looking to another human being to fix the need and the pain inside of me. Forgive me for having sought satisfaction and fulfillment from anyone other than you. I now loose, cut, and sever any and all soul ties I have willingly or ignorantly entered into. I reject these soul ties and every soulish satisfaction they have provided for me. I detach them from myself, I renounce them, and I will turn away from every wrong agreements I came into that birthed the soul ties in the first place. I've tried too long and too unsuccessfully to get my own soulish, human expectations fulfilled. Increase my awareness of the fallibility of my expectations. Increase my awareness of old patterns of behavior I need to loose. Increase my awareness of wrong thinking I need to loose and reject. Increase my awareness. In Jesus' name."

Resources for Overcoming Masturbation:

The best article I have read on masturbation is by Mike and Jody Cleveland and entitled "Masturbation– a Doorway to Slavery" and can be obtained by emailing Mike at: webservant@settingcaptivesfree.com

Resources for Dating:

The best book I am aware of for determining how compatible you are with someone you are dating is by Barbara DeAngelis entitled *Are You the One for Me?* It is not a faith–based book; however, it is excellent. Her book covers topics such as: falling in love for the wrong reasons, the ten types of relationships that won't work, fatal flaws, and six qualities to look for in a mate. Barbara's compatibility test encompasses: physical style, emotional style, social style, intellectual style, communication style, professional/financial style, personal growth style, spiritual style, and interests/hobbies.

Date...or Soul Mate? How to Know If Someone Is Worth Pursuing In Two Dates Or Less" by Neil Clark Warren, Ph.D.

I Kissed Dating Goodbye by Joshua Harris—boundaries for dating

The Hard Questions: 100 *Essential Questions to Ask Before You Say "I Do*" by Susan Piver.

www.asianfriendfinder.com Christian Dating Tips

www.adammeeteve.com "Why God says not to have sex outside of marriage." Pastor Jim Reeves

http://teenadvice.about.com/cs/whatislove/ht/areyouinloveht.htm "How to know it's love"

Resources for Overcoming Same–sex Attraction:

www.settingcaptivesfree.com—free online course for overcoming homosexuality, porn addiction, and masturbation

Exodus Ministries www.exodus–international.org., www.newdirection.ca

"Out of Egypt" and accompanying workbook by Jeanette Howard (overcoming lesbianism)

"Pursuing Sexual Wholeness" (workbook also available)— Andrew Comiskey

"My Spouse is Gay: Finding Help for a Troubled Marriage"— Anita Worthen and Bob Davies

"The Broken Image"—Leanne Payne

"Coming Out of Homosexuality"—Bob Davies and Lori Rentzel

"Homosexual No More"—Dr. William Consiglio

Other books: http://hawebpage.truepath.com/book/list/resourcea.html

EFFECTS OF ABUSE

It is difficult for many people who have been abused as a child or as an adult to understand how a loving God could allow something so horrendous to happen to them. The fact is that He gave people free will and people choose to sin. I believe God weeps when people are abused, especially powerless children.

Healing Abusive Childhoods

Biblical Principles to Understand from the book Shared Grace: Therapists and Clergy Working Together[33]:

- God is love.

- God loves us (you).

- God's love is unconditional (for you).

- God's forgiveness is always available to us (for you).

- We are called to love God, ourselves, and others.

- We were created to be in relationship with one another.

Goals[34]

1. Build trust in oneself and in others.

2. Create a sense of safety in the world.

3. Create a new worldview.

4. Develop life–coping skills.

5. Develop healing images of God so that you can establish a healthy, personal relationship with God.

Understanding how a Loving God could Allow such Abuse

It is understandable that if you suffered abuse as an innocent child, that you could be angry and resentful toward God for allowing such abuse. You did nothing to deserve what happened to you. God understands your anger; it is okay to express your feelings, even all the negatives ones, to Him. He knows how you feel and what you think anyway, and He still accepts you just as you are. You may need to express those emotions to Him before you are ready to see Him in a different light, but at some point, it will be important to know and understand the truth about God.

Read what one survivor of horrific abuse as a child wrote in *Shared Grace*[35] "God is not my personal bodyguard, there to fight those who would hurt me. I have come to believe that God was deeply saddened by the abuse of my mother and wept for me. While God did not come down from the mount riding a white horse as I would have liked, God did provide places and people at some well–chosen times in my life so that I would not go completely insane. God gave the strength to hold on until

I could find a therapist who would help me. I had seen many therapists before I found one that I felt safe with and now I see that she was one of the greatest gifts that God could have given me. While I would have not chosen the abuse for myself, I also realize that without having experienced the abuse, I would not be who I am today."

Try to imagine some painful memories as a child and picture how God would be weeping at such treatment, how it would break His heart to see you in so much pain. He was always there and always cared, and even though He had to allow it due to man's free will, He never wished it. He desperately wanted to stop it. But He also knew you would survive it and be healed, and that He could bring good out of such a terrible situation. He knew it would be temporary and He knew that the love you did not receive then as a child would be magnified a thousand times over and given to you later when you were able to receive His love, His pure love, His unconditional love, a much better love.

Even if you can't think of ways that God was actually trying to help you back then, try to think of areas where you did feel God's presence or when you have experienced God's grace in some way. Even a lack of memories could be seen as a "gift" of God. Similarly, there may have been people placed in your life—a grandparent, a teacher, a friend—who helped ease the pain and suffering in some way. Such images, over time, help to counteract images of God as uncaring.

Remember, too, that God allowed His own beloved son, Jesus, to be abused. He allowed him to be born in a barn and considered as illegitimate. He was rejected and misunderstood, abandoned by friends, betrayed by a disciple, experienced grief at the loss of loved ones, and so forth. Then, he was beaten, mocked, whipped, and crucified on the cross. Can you see, though, that God allowed Jesus to endure this suffering, shame, and mistreatment because it would result in salvation for thousands upon thousands? Countless people will know joy, peace, a right relationship with God, and a home in heaven, and so much more because of Jesus' suffering.

I can imagine God weeping while He saw them crucify His son, but He knew it had to be allowed for a greater good for many. In the same way, He felt heartache to see you being abused but He knew that He could bring much good out of it, and He will—if we let Him do His work in and through us.

Jesus knew he was going to experience great suffering and the death of his body but He willingly went through it all because He knew, even though He might not have totally comprehended it all at the time, that he could trust His loving Father, even to allow abuse of that magnitude. We need to always know, in spite of our past or present circumstances, that He is a loving God who will only allow bad things to happen to us for loving and good reasons.

While it is understandable to feel disappointed and perplexed by our circumstances, we are not disappointed in God. We remind ourselves that He sees the whole big picture while we can only see the part that we are presently experiencing. God, who sees the future, knows what is best for today and we trust in His wisdom, in His goodness, and in His character.

How can we accept God the Father as loving when our earthly parents were abusive?

Although God is referred to as the "Father" in the Bible with parental attributes, we need to understand that, at the same time, God is very different from earthly parents.[36]

Earthly parents	God as parent
– can be abusive	– is never abusive
– can be unloving and cruel	– always loves unconditionally
– may punish in anger	– teaches in love
– may not have the child's best interests at heart	– always has our best interests at heart
– wrong motivation	– always motivated by love toward us
– impatient	– always patient and understanding
– may neglect or abandon their own children	– will never leave us or abandon us
– may be unpredictable	– can always be counted on as loving
– may not be concerned with children's well–being	– always concerned with our well–being
– may be unforgiving	– always forgiving

– add any others you can think of

Seeing God differently

"God is represented in Jesus, and everything Jesus does is a reflection of God. God had to become human to communicate who God is and what God is like. What then, does the Bible teach us about Jesus? We never find Jesus abusing people in the Bible, quite the contrary. In the book of Luke, Jesus is depicted as reaching out to the poor, the outcasts, the wounded. To these people, his response is mercy and compassion."[37]

And that is how Jesus sees you, with mercy, compassion, and unfailing love. He is the shepherd of the sheep, gently guiding them, bringing back the strays with love, protecting them constantly, watching over them continuously, keeping them safe, taking care of them, meeting all their needs. And, so He does with you.

How can I ever feel safe?

It would appear to a child that God had abandoned him/her, and that there really is no safety in the world. True safety does not exist in the absence of danger, but is found in the truth that God has not abandoned us, no matter what we have done, no matter what has happened to us. We cannot hide or run away from all the dangers of the world. Sometimes bad things will happen, and we cannot look to God to prevent them.

A true sense of safety in the world can only come when we no longer experience God as uncaring or vengeful and punitive, but as present and always loving toward us. When we truly understand God's loving and caring nature, we will feel safe because we will know that even if something bad is allowed to happen in our lives, that He is still a loving and caring God that has allowed those circumstances for a loving and good reason. Therein lies true security.

But it's still so hard for me to trust God[38]

"Although we may never understand why bad things have happened to us, when we have healed our images of God, we can trust that ultimately, we will be okay. This sense that we will be okay no matter what happens relates to having faith."

When I think of having faith, I always think of the image of the little boy who is in a burning house. The family has escaped, but the father notices that one child, a little boy, has been left behind. The house is blazing and the father cannot go back in to find him. All of a sudden, his son appears at a second story window from which smoke is billowing. He yells, "Jump, Son. I will catch you." The little boy cannot see a thing because of the smoke, so he yells, "But Dad, I can't see you!" Dad implores: "Jump, Son!" The little boy replies again: "But Dad, I can't see you!" to which the Dad says "But *I* can see *you*." That whole image of having faith is like the child jumping out the window when he does not really know for sure his father is going to be there to catch him. Having faith then, is trusting that God is going to be there."

Meaning in Suffering

"No matter why abuse has occurred, the problems and symptoms that have resulted from that experience of abuse can be viewed as opportunities for emotional and spiritual growth. We need to reject the idea that we are victims and move beyond the blame, the pain, the guilt and shame, toward hope for the future."[39]

A Jewish survivor of the Holocaust and a German prison camp, for example, chose to find some good out of that horrific experience. He was able to transform the meaning of the abuse and killing into something other than terror, horror, and hatred. That transformation came as he forgave his oppressors. How could he, having seen innocent people suffer and die at the hands of the Nazis, having suffered so greatly himself, find it in his heart to forgive, to even thank his oppressors for providing the opportunity to grow?

Forgiveness for the survivor involves letting go of the pain so that it does not keep you from being happy now. It does not mean letting the abuser off the hook, so that the abuser does not have to accept responsibility for what was done. Nor does forgiving imply forgetting the abuse ever occurred.

Forgiveness is a process that has its own timetable, its own course; however, you will continue to remain a victim until you are ready to forgive. You stay the abuser's victim and they still have power over you because you cannot be healed totally and move on until you forgive. If it takes some time to truly forgive and you are still harbouring anger, God is patient and understanding; however, He wants you to be at peace and to be free from the effects of the abuse, and so He will patiently wait for you to complete your healing through forgiveness.

Letter to your abuser

Before one can forgive someone who has abused them, they should have every opportunity to thoroughly explore all the ways that the abuse affected them at the time and all the ways it continues to impact them. This is a painful process that can cause emotional upheaval and can bring back bad memories but worth the process to finally work through it and then move forward.

We naturally suppress some negative memories and yet most survivors of abuse have some vague recollections that come to mind from time to time. One way to help to restore memories is by accessing your memories by trying to remember through your senses. So, in other words, at the time, what did you see? What could you smell? What sounds were present or what words were spoken? What did you feel by touch? What did you think/feel at the time?

Once you are more in touch with the memory by senses, start examining and exploring all the ways the abuse affected you. It could be you lost your sense of personal safety or you lost your ability to trust others. You may have lost your child-hood innocence forever. What core beliefs did you develop as a result of the abuse? That no one can be trusted? That this is not a safe world? That you are bad? That you must have deserved it and it was your fault?

Then look at how the abuse has affected you since. Has it affected your trust level in relationships? How has it impacted on your self–esteem? How did it change your self–image?

Write a letter to the abuser that you don't actually intend to give or send. This is your chance to express every feeling and thought– all the sadness, confusion, fear, shame, anger, whatever. Pour it all out in the letter. Talk to God about it as well and ask Him to heal you of the effects of the abuse and to heal those memories. Once you feel you have thoroughly dealt with how the abuse affected you, then throw the letter away or destroy it as a symbol of "letting go" of the pain of it and letting go of the past. Then you begin your forgiveness work.

The truth is that if someone took advantage of you and you were not completely consenting, then they were a perpetrator and you were a victim. They committed a crime and you didn't deserve it and it *wasn't* your fault and they deserve to bear the consequences and be held accountable for their actions.

What about confronting or reporting the abuser to the authorities?

I often get asked by my counseling clients if they should confront their abuser but it really depends on the individual situation. For example, if someone sexually abused you and you know where that person lives and their name, you can choose to report them to the police or Children's Services if you were a child at the time.

There are three main reasons for reporting the abuse. The person did commit a crime against you and should be judged in a court of law and dealt with accordingly. The second reason is that sexual offenders often go on to repeat their offences, especially pedophiles, and if no one reports their crimes, then other people/children may be abused as well. If you suspect the perpetrator may abuse someone else, then you have an obligation to report them unless that will jeopardize your own safety.

Finally, it is a way of you regaining control over your life and declaring that they were to blame—you were mistreated and that was wrong. It is saying that you are worthy of respect and dignity and that they need to be held accountable for their actions.

What if the abuser was someone you know or a family member? Then you have to ask yourself what will be accomplished to confront that family member based on how well you know the person and what kind of response you can expect to receive from them. Unfortunately, some abusers continue to deny the abuse so if you are going to confront them, you need to be prepared for any response. It helps if another person supports you in the confrontation, but you really need to weigh how much this would benefit you.

Some people may feel that it is worth it just so they have their say and can tell the person how wrong it was and how hurt they were by the person's behaviour, but you can also do this in a letter you don't deliver and by telling other people or praying through it with the Lord. If you have worked through it already and you know the person is not at risk of abusing anyone else or not likely to, then make confronting them a serious matter of prayer.

It may not even be safe for you to speak to the abuser directly so a lot of things need to be carefully weighed out. It would be wonderful if survivors could approach their abusers and the response was genuine remorse and the relationship was then healed and restored, and that can happen, but unless you really believe they are going to respond that way, there is a lot to consider.

There is a Web site at www.red–letters.com where people post anonymous letters to their abuser, which is another option. You may need to seek professional help to get in touch with your feelings and work through abuse you have suffered. As horrible as the abuse was, you can always strive to bring good out of any situation. Perhaps the Lord would want you to minister to others who have been abused once you have experienced sufficient healing for yourself.

Resources for Overcoming the Effects of the Past:

Unlocking the Secrets of Your Childhood Memories—Randy Carlson

Changes that Heal: How to Understand Your Past to Ensure a Healthier Future—Henry Cloud

Spiritual Warfare for the Wounded—Mark Johnson

Healing of Memories—David A. Seamands

Beyond Tolerable Recovery—Ed Smith

Reclaiming Your Inner Child—Ken Parker

Putting Away Childish Things—David A. Seamands

Helping Victims of Sexual Abuse—Jeanette Vought and Lynn Heitritter

Hope for the Brokenhearted: Biblical Solutions for Survivors of Abuse and Rape—Todd R. Cook

GRIEF

After the loss of eight relatives including both my parents, this subject is one that is close to my heart. Most of the deaths of my family members were the result of common diseases such as cancer and heart failure; however, the more difficult grief work for me came as a result of two suicides, a thirty–two– year–old cousin who died of Aids (which he got from a woman) and a thirty–eight– year–old cousin who died as a result of an eating disorder. I also lost a dear friend, Margaret, who died at the age of forty. This chapter is in honor of Margaret.

Definitions

The term bereavement refers to the element of loss experienced by a loved one's passing and it describes many types of loss: the loss of a relationship, loss of a role, loss of a sense of control, loss of security, loss of an orderly world view, etc. Grief is the personal response to loss that includes physical, psychological, emotional, social, and spiritual components. Mourning is more about the process of the readjustment of one's life without the deceased through grief work.

Traumatic loss or complicated grief refers to a loss producing immediate or delayed stress along with significant physical, psychological, emotional, spiritual, and/or social changes. There might be problems with the expression of grief, people may have distorted beliefs about the grief, and they may appear "stuck" in the grief process. Traumatic losses may include sudden/unexpected deaths or violent deaths or when one unexpectedly finds the body of a loved one. The shock may result in panic, helplessness, and/or may overwhelm the individual's ability to cope so the grief reaction is beyond the range of normal human experience.

A grief that a person experiences that cannot be openly acknowledged, publicly mourned, or socially supported is known as disenfranchised grief. Examples would be the death of a loved one due to AIDS, an eating disorder, or suicide.

Physical Reactions

Someone suffering from grief may experience any number of physiological responses such as: disturbances in sleep, eating behaviours, nausea, headaches, trembling, and fatigue. Always check with your physician to rule out any physical causes.

Psychological Reactions

After losing a loved one, you may experience difficulties with concentration, memory, confusion, preoccupation with the deceased and the cause of death, and unpredictable mood swings—you may even fear you are "losing it." Other psychological symptoms of grief are: apathy, irrational lashing out at family members and friends, and sometimes a desire to escape to another place, time, especially to past times.

Emotional Reactions

One can be overwhelmed with any number of emotions after the loss of loved one: shock, numbing, sadness, anxiety, anger, guilt, fear, vulnerability, an obsession with honouring the memory of the past (a need to write about the circumstances surrounding the death for example), or wallowing in memories that contribute to pain. Often guilt feelings surface; people think "if only" they did this differently or "if only" this took place, and so forth. The truth is if there is nothing you could have done that would have changed the outcome, then that guilt is irrational; forgive yourself, accept God's forgiveness, make improvements where possible, and move forward.

Behavioural Reactions

There may be a compulsion to revisit places/events associated with the loss. You might think for a moment that you see the person in familiar places.

Spiritual Reactions

A significant loss often results in a re–evaluation of one's beliefs. Death triggers awareness of our own mortality and we search for meaning in the loss. We may go through periods when we are angry with God or we may at times feel that we cannot trust God. It is important to have a consistent, Christian support system in place during this time. Make an appointment to speak with your pastor or Christian counsellor if you need to discuss the ways the loss has affected your relationship with God.

The death of a loved one can bring about social changes as well. There might be a loss of role (daughter, parent, sibling, etc.) or social isolation. The loss may also trigger disturbances in relationships.

The Stages of Dealing with Grief

Grief and loss are inevitable and universal. The finality of death results in severe emotional pain. We grieve for loved ones who have passed on, but we can also grieve for the end of a relationship (divorce) or we can suffer the same emotional reactions over the loss of a beloved pet. Other losses include: loss of employment, loss of health, loss of financial security, loss of the familiar, loss of status, etc. Grieving is difficult because it involves many intense feelings that can be disorienting and last over a long period of time. Bereavement has often been described as drowning in a sea of painful emotions. I often think of a Native expression I once heard to describe the grief one feels as "my heart is on the ground."

Dr. Elizabeth Kubler–Ross is renowned for her stages of death: shock/denial, anger, bargaining, depression, and acceptance; however, because grief is such an individual thing, you may find yourself skipping some of the stages and/or revisiting other stages.

Shock is usually the first stage immediately following the death of a loved on. You may even feel that you are "in a fog," which can last a few days or for several months if it was a traumatic death of someone very close to you. There is also an emotional reaction when you truly realize the depth of the loss. You may cry profusely or you may feel you are "losing it" because you are unable to manage the usual daily functions, or you keep forgetting things and feel disoriented.

It is a normal response to experience guilt over not doing enough for the deceased or you might feel guilty in relation to events surrounding the loved one's death.

At some point, you may get good and angry toward whoever or whatever you believe "caused" the death of your loved one. You may go back and forth through these reactions for some time; however, eventually you will come to the point of acceptance when you are able to readjust to your life without that person in it. You yield to a new phase in your life and start looking ahead. It will never be the same without your loved one but you begin to cherish the memories of your interaction with that person.

There is no set timeline for how long it takes anyone to come to the point of acceptance and moving forward. It depends on how close you were to the person who died, how they died, your relationship with them at the end, and your own coping strategies. For a difficult death, it may take a few years to feel that you are back to your "normal" self again. The first Christmas and special anniversaries will be particularly difficult, such as the first birthday without the loved one, the first Mother's Day, and so forth.

Grieving is difficult work. The following are some suggestions to help you in managing the journey through grief.

Don'ts:

- Don't let others rush you into recovery from grief. (If someone tells you to "get over it," find another friend.)

- Don't make major decisions; the time of grief is a time of vulnerability and uncertainty.

- Don't attempt to escape/bury/numb negative feelings with the use of alcohol or drugs.

Dos:

- Cry to release the pain; don't hold back crying for the sake of others.

- Keep busy, do work that has a purpose, do activities that involve your mind and concentration.

- Look over photographs and any other mementos that remind you of your loved one. Reminisce with family members or friends.

- Seek out people who will really listen to you, especially those who have experienced a similar loss in the past.

- Deal with guilt, real or imagined. Accept the fact that you are not perfect and if you have asked God for forgiveness, then you are forgiven.

- Allow yourself time to heal. Pay attention to self–care. Make sure you are getting enough sleep. Try to eat a healthy diet and get regular exercise, even if going for a short walk every day.

- Nuture yourself every day. Try to do something good for yourself. Think of what you might do for someone else if they were in your shoes and do it for yourself.

- Ask for help when needed. Now is not the time to try to manage everything by yourself.

- Establish new routines/habits to replace ones you did together (go to a new store to get groceries, for example).

Record your thoughts in a journal. It may help you to articulate your feelings and may demonstrate your healing progress. Sometimes it is helpful to write a letter to the deceased person. In the letter, express all your thoughts and feelings about their passing and how it is affecting you. If you weren't able to say whatever you would have wanted to before their passing, say it to them now. Other people prefer to just speak to the deceased loved one as if they were in the room. You can also share your pain with the Lord in prayer.

When you are ready, there are many ways to honour the memory of the deceased person. You can make a shoebox that you decorate and fill with special mementos of your relationship with that person. You can create a photo/video tribute, put an ad in the paper, or add their name to a memory garden/wall. On Christmas or special days, put their photo in a prominent place and light a candle beside it to include them. At a wedding, place their photo and/or a candle in their memory near the altar. You can also create a memorial on www.stillremember.com.

You don't have to cope with your loss on your own. Grief counselling is available through community resources, churches, and licensed therapists. Join a grief support group. Local community papers will usually have listings. Use the Internet and join an online support group. (www.angel–on–my–shoulder. com is a good Christian site.)

Healing takes time. If the loss was profound and the emotional wound very deep, there may be a permanent scar on your heart, but the memories of the loved one will always be there as well.

Remember, there is no right way or wrong way to grieve. People grieve in their own time and in their own way. The feeling of grief can often be like the feeling of fear, as observed by C. S. Lewis in his book *A Grief Observed*, "No one ever told me that grief felt so like fear." So everything you feel during bereavement is normal for you.

Grief is the pain of not having the person who is gone. Through bereavement we learn to live without that person and in the words of St. John Chrysostorn, a bishop living in the fourth century, "He whom we love and lose is no longer where he was before. He is now wherever we are." No one can take away or stop your love or your memories or the interaction you had with that person. That doesn't die and never will.

You may wish to consult with your pastor or Christian counsellor to help with making sense of the loss in terms of personal beliefs, confrontation with your own personal mortality, and to discuss any ways that the loss has affected your relationship with God.

Of course, as Christians, whether or not our loved ones went to heaven is another issue. While it is a great comfort to think of a loved one in heaven, their presence on earth will still be missed. The thought of a loved one going to hell is a little too painful for our hearts and minds to fully grasp, thank God. If we know a loved one died without knowing the Lord; however, it should be impetus for us to witness to others in our lives while we have the time and opportunities to do so.

Grief Can Become a Problem When:

- Your physical health is affected because you are not eating or sleeping enough or you are becoming ill often because your immune system is lowered.

- You cannot carry out your normal daily activities.

- You have isolated yourself from others to the point where you are alone most of the time and not even communicating with others on the phone.

- You find yourself over–medicating or drinking excessively in an effort to deal with the pain.

Seek professional help if you are experiencing any of the above or if you have experienced traumatic loss, disenfranchised grief, and/or complicated grief. Deaths that involve suicide, murder, and the loss of a child are particularly difficult. Ask God how He can bring something good out of these horrific and painful losses. I am reminded of a missionary couple that lost all six of their children but as a result they started up an orphanage for children. The mother of a child that was killed by a drunk driver started MADD–Mothers Against Drunk Driving. John Walsh from America's Most Wanted began the TV show that has been responsible for the capture and incarceration of many criminals because his son, Adam, was brutally murdered.

Several translations of the Bible mention Jesus telling Mary Magdalene to let go of him. "Do not hold on to me, do not cling to me" (John 20:17). We have to let go. Saying good–bye to our loved ones, however, doesn't end the love we hold for them or the love they held in their hearts for us. Eventually, you will be able to be thankful for the period of time that you did have the person in your life.

Revelation 21:4, "And God shall wipe away all tears from their eyes; and there shall be no more death, neither sorrow, nor crying, neither shall there be any more pain: for the former things are passed away."

Miscarriage/Abortion

Losing a baby, even a pre–born one, can be a significant loss. It may help to name the child. It is important that you are able to talk about this loss with someone who understands how painful this loss can be.

If you had an abortion and have asked God for forgiveness, then you are forgiven. Don't keep Jesus on the cross by not accepting His sacrifice for this and by not forgiving yourself. Many women deal with the guilt of having an abortion and they grieve too.

Again, it can be helpful if you have a sense of whether the baby was a boy or a girl and if you can think of a name for him/her. You can carry out some sort of ceremony to commemorate the loss. You can talk to the child and tell him/her how you feel.

Know, too, that you will see your children in heaven. I knew a woman in Toronto who had three abortions and when she got saved, the Lord showed her those children and she received

His forgiveness and she now has a ministry to women who have had abortions.

Pet Loss

The loss of a beloved pet can be just as painful as losing a close family member. Animals, especially dogs, love their owners unconditionally and it would be impossible to spend so much time interacting with your pet and not feel a tremendous loss when they are gone. Give yourself permission to grieve your pet and get support from others who have had a similar loss. You can post a tribute to your pet at http://www.in–memory–of–pets.com.

Have you heard the lyrics to the song "If You Could See Me Now" by Kim Noblitt? It paints a picture of your loved one in heaven, sitting at Jesus' feet, walking the streets of gold, with no more pain, and so forth. If you could see your loved one, you would know that they would never want to leave heaven. It doesn't mean you won't miss them dearly until you are reunited with them, but it may help ease the pain because you can appreciate that you want the best for them and they have that now.

Another poem from the loved one's perspective is "My First Christmas in Heaven" written by Wanda Bencke who lost her thirteen–year–old daughter, which can be read at http://www.christmasinheaven.net/christmas.html.

Then there is this poem posted on the wall at the Oklahoma City bombing site by K.C. and Myke Kuzmic from Stockton, California:

As I prayed, I said, "God, I hurt." And God said, "I know."

I said, "God, I cry a lot." And God said, "That is why I gave you tears."

I said, "God, I am so depressed." And God said, "That is why I gave you sunshine."

I said, "God, life is so hard." And God said, "That is why I gave you loved ones."

I said, "God, my loved one died." And God said, "So did mine."

I said, "God, it is such a loss." And God said, "I saw mine nailed to a cross."

I said, "God, but your loved one lives." And God said, "So does yours."

I said, "God, where are they now?" And God said, "Mine is on My right and yours is in the Light."

I said, "God, I miss them." And God said, "I know. But worry not, for the second coming of mine is close at hand."

There is also a wonderful poem by David M. Romano called "If Tomorrow Starts Without Me." He speaks of how the loved one is finally content with God in heaven and ends his poem with, "So when tomorrow starts without me, Don't think we're far apart, for every time you think of me, I'm right here in your heart."

Resources:

www.Bible.ca has a biblical study of "In Overcoming Grief" by Gerry Trickle.

Finding Hope Again—Neil Anderson

Pearls: Scriptures to Live By—Brian Campbell

Creative Suffering—Paul Tournier

Grief Counselling & Grief Therapy—William J. Worden

Recovering from the Losses of Life—Norman H. Wright

A Grief Observed—C.S. Lewis

"Living in His Forgiveness" by Sandy Day and is written
to help post–abortive women find grace, forgiveness, and
freedom.

Online Grief Support Classes—www.griefsteps.com

http://www.griefsupportservices.org/newgrief/griefsupports-
ervices/onlinesupportgroup.php (online grief support groups)

Sexual Addiction

Childhood sexual abuse may be a contributing factor to adult sexual addiction; however, it may also be due to the gradual surrender to sexual fantasy, masturbation, and the viewing of pornography. Contributing emotional factors are low self–esteem and feeling rejected/dejected or undesirable. You may have decided to meet your needs for comfort and good feelings in your own way because you do not trust God or others to meet your emotional needs. Your method of coping with not feeling loved may have developed into a habit of sexual gratification.

Inevitably, you will realize that you only feel better for a very short period of time and then you may get overwhelmed with shame and guilt and feel powerless to overcome the patterns you have developed. There is a cyclical chemical reaction that takes place in the brain when masturbation is combined with pornography, which makes it an extremely powerful addiction to overcome.[40]

Yet we know that with God nothing is impossible. I often refer my online counselling clients who are addicted to porn to www.settingcaptivesfree.com. They can sign up for a free online course that is biblically–based and they are assigned a mentor to pray for them, support them, and so forth. Of course, it isn't effective if the person doesn't log on to the site and answer the questions every day so it is of utmost importance that you determine to overcome this problem once and for all. Expect a few setbacks, but always get right back on track as soon as possible.

One of their concepts dealing with porn addiction is "radical amputation," in other words, steer clear of any and all triggers that prompt you to start thinking about sex. So, for example, if you frequently go to a store that has x–rated magazines in a prominent place, determine to go to other stores for whatever you need, even if it is out of the way. Put a filter on your computer and, if necessary, get rid of cable channels on your TV, or dispose of your TV altogether! The idea is to remove as many temptation triggers for you as possible.

Another approach emphasized in the online course at www.settingcaptivesfree.com is to encourage you to develop the strong relationship with the Lord that you need so that you look to Him to provide all your needs instead of giving in to the flesh. Look to God for your comfort, for improved self–esteem, and to feel loved.

Experts say that it takes a minimum of twenty–one days to change a behavior but it often takes even longer to completely overcome porn addiction. The online course is for sixty consecutive days and some people have to complete the course more than once to get complete victory, so have patience with yourself, but keep working at it. Write down your goal and make a list of activities that you can do instead whenever you get the urge to participate in sinful activity. Get up and leave the house and go for a run, do crossword puzzles or something else that fully engages your concentration, phone a friend—whatever works for you.

Be aware of when you are most vulnerable to giving in to temptation, when you are tired, bored, depressed, stressed out, or disappointed. Make sure you get the support you need during those times. It is also vital to set up some kind of accountability system. Get your spouse or a Christian friend to hold you accountable and check up on your progress. Ask them to pray with you when tempted. Some churches even have men's groups for men addicted to porn and women's groups for wives of husbands addicted to porn. Why not see if there is a need at your church and start such a group?

It is not always men addicted to porn and masturbation. I have had several women clients who have the same issues, and what's more, I have discovered that often women who view a lot of pornography can often develop same–sex attraction, which they also need to overcome.

There is a temptation to rationalize our sins involving sexual addiction. It is so easy to say that God gave you the physical urges and it is only natural or that you need to release emotional tension or that most people do it or whatever. Others claim that because it is not specifically named in the Bible that it is not a big deal or the matter is open to interpretation.

The truth is that anything that makes us a slave to the flesh so that we are not submitted to the Holy Spirit, is significantly affecting our spiritual growth and our fellowship with God. If you are not convinced that masturbation is sinful, I would recommend that you read Mike Cleveland's article "Masturbation– a Doorway to Slavery" and it can be obtained by emailing Mike at webservant@settingcaptivesfree.com. Sexual addiction is rarely overcome on one's own.

Does My Spouse Have A Problem?
By Rory Reid & Dan Gray[41]

Determining whether or not there is a pornography problem is a careful balancing act. Some spouses dismiss behaviour that should be confronted due to incomplete or insufficient information. One woman, despite her frustration and disgust, excused her husband's pornography habit because she inaccurately assumed it was part of normal male behaviour. When his habit later led to a cyber affair, she expressed regret about not confronting the behaviour sooner.

Another woman grew suspicious of her husband's late–night computer activities, which he said were "work related." Rather than expressing her concern she quietly went to bed each night. A few months later she discovered her suspicions were accurate and her husband had been viewing pornography. Both these examples represent situations where more information should have been gathered and behaviour should have been confronted.

Signs of an Existing Problem:

Often, suspicions arise long before an inappropriate behaviour is discovered. There are several signs that may indicate a problem with pornography or other behaviours related to sexual addiction. These signs may include:

- Loss of interest in sexual relations or insatiable sexual appetite

- Introduction of unusual sexual practices in the relationship

- Diminished emotional, physical, social, spiritual, and intellectual intimacy

- Neglect of responsibilities

- Increased isolation (such as late–night hours on the computer) or withdrawal from family

- Easily irritated, irregular mood swings

- Unexplained absences

- Preference for masturbation over sexual relations with spouse

- Unexplained financial transactions

- Sexual relations that are rigid, without passion, and detached

If these signs are present in a marriage, it is possible there is a pornography–related problem.

Resources for Overcoming Sexual Addiction:

If you are not sure if you have a sexual addiction problem, there are many self–tests such as www.sexaddictionhelp.com/test.html

www.settingcaptivesfree.com—free alcohol, overeating, same-sex attraction and pornography/masturbation online courses with an assigned mentor. Also provides the "Pure Freedom Mentor's Guide" if you want to lead a group for men addicted to porn. Also available at www.christianbook.com.

www.purelifeministries.com—overcoming pornography addiction.

www.contentwatch.com—porn filter for your computer and a scan to discover porn on it.

Books on pornography and sites
for wives of men addicted to porn

The Excellent Wife—Martha Peace
(www.marthapeace.com)

Intimate Issues—Lorraine Pintus
(www.intimateissues.com)

Through Deep Waters by Kathy Gallagher

Discussing Pornography Problems with a Spouse—
Rory Reid and Dan Gray

Chemical Addictions

The first part of drug and alcohol addiction begins when you make it a habit to take a pill or a drink to meet your need for emotional comfort or support. You begin to rely on this method of coping in your life. As your tolerance increases over time, it takes more and more to get the same initial high. At this point you are feeling guilty and powerless and other people around you are becoming concerned for you. You begin to withdraw and start going places where people don't know you.

John Hopkins University Hospital in Baltimore, Maryland offers this self–assessment known as the Cage test to determine if you have a drinking problem:

1. Do you lose time from work due to drinking?

2. Is drinking making your life unhappy?

3. Do you drink because you are shy with other people?

4. Is drinking affecting your reputation?

5. Have you ever felt remorse after drinking?

6. Have you gotten into financial difficulties because of drinking?

7. Do you turn to lower companions and an inferior environment when drinking?

8. Does drinking make you careless of your family's welfare?

9. Has your ambition decreased since drinking?

10. Do you crave a drink at a definite time daily?

11. Do you want a drink the next morning?

12. Does drinking cause you to have difficulty sleeping?

13. Has your efficiency decreased since drinking?

14. Is drinking jeopardizing your job or business?

15. Do you drink to escape from worries or trouble?

16. Do you drink alone?

17. Have you ever had a complete loss of memory as a result of drinking?

18. Has your physician ever treated you for drinking?

19. Do you drink to build up your self–confidence?

20. Have you ever been to a hospital or institution on account of drinking?

If you answer yes to any one of these questions, it is a definite warning sign that you may be an alcoholic. If you answer yes to any two questions, you are most likely an alcoholic, and if you answer yes to three or more, you are undoubtedly an alcoholic.

As with gambling or sexual addiction, you must first admit that you have a problem. You need to learn how to look to God to meet your needs and to overcome well-established thinking/behavioural patterns. This will require total dependence on God and the support of others.

Gambling Addiction

"Compulsive gambling is an illness, progressive in its nature, which can never be cured, but can be arrested. Just as an alcoholic has to avoid alcohol at all costs for the rest of his/her life, it is the same with gambling."[42]

What are some characteristics of a person who is a compulsive gambler?

1. Inability and unwillingness to accept reality—hence the escape into the dream world of gambling.

2. Emotional insecurity. A compulsive gambler finds he or she is emotionally comfortable only when "in action." It is not uncommon to hear a Gamblers Anonymous member say: "The only place I really felt like I belonged was sitting at the poker table. There I felt secure and comfortable. No great demands were made upon me. I knew I was destroy-

ing myself, yet at the same time, I had a certain sense of security."

3. Immaturity. A desire to have all the good things in life without any great effort on their part seems to be the common character pattern of problem gamblers. Many Gamblers Anonymous members accept the fact that they were unwilling to grow up. Subconsciously they felt they could avoid mature responsibility by wagering on the spin of a wheel or the turn of a card, and so the struggle to escape responsibility finally became a subconscious obsession.

Also, a compulsive gambler seems to have a strong inner urge to be a "big shot" and needs to have a feeling of being all powerful. The compulsive gambler is willing to do anything (often of an anti-social nature) to maintain the image he or she wants others to see.

Then, too, there is a theory that compulsive gamblers subconsciously want to lose to punish themselves. There is much evidence to support this theory. Gamblers Anonymous offers the following questions to anyone who may have a gambling problem. These questions are provided to help the individual decide if he or she is a compulsive gambler and wants to stop gambling. Gamblers Anonymous offers this self–assessment for gambling addiction:

Twenty Questions

1. Did you ever lose time from work or school due to gambling?

2. Has gambling ever made your home life unhappy?

3. Did gambling affect your reputation?

4. Have you ever felt remorse after gambling?

5. Did gambling ever cause a decrease in your ambition or efficiency?

6. After losing did you feel you must return as soon as possible and win back your losses?

7. After a win did you have a strong urge to return and win more?

8. Did you often gamble until your last dollar was gone?

9. Did you ever borrow to finance your gambling?

10. Have you ever sold anything to finance gambling?

11. Were you reluctant to use "gambling money" for normal expenditures?

12. Did gambling make you careless of the welfare of yourself and your family?

13. Did you ever gamble longer than you had planned?

14. Have you ever gambled to escape worry or trouble?

15. Ever committed, or considered committing, an illegal act to finance gambling?

16. Did gambling ever cause you to have difficulty sleeping?

17. Do arguments, disappointments, or frustrations create an urge to gamble?

18. Did you ever have an urge to celebrate any good fortune by gambling?

19. Have you ever considered self–destruction as a result of your gambling?

20. Did you ever gamble to get money with which to pay debts or otherwise solve financial difficulties?

Steps of a 12 Step Program of Recovery—We:

1. Admitted we were powerless over gambling, that our lives had become unmanageable.

2. Came to believe that a Power greater than ourselves could restore us to a normal way of thinking and living.

3. Made a decision to turn our will and our lives over to the care of this Power of our own understanding.

4. Made a searching and fearless moral and financial inventory of ourselves.

5. Admitted to ourselves and to another human being the exact nature of our wrongs.

6. Were entirely ready to have these defects of character removed.

7. Humbly asked God (of our understanding) to remove our shortcomings.

8. Made a list of all persons we had harmed and became willing to make amends to them all.

9. Make direct amends to such people wherever possible, except when to do so would injure them or others.

10. Continued to take personal inventory and when we were wrong, promptly admitted it.

11. Sought through prayer and meditation to improve our conscious contact with God as we understood Him, praying only for knowledge of His will for us and the power to carry that out.

12. Having made an effort to practice these principles in all our affairs, we tried to carry this message to other compulsive gamblers, alcoholics, drug addicts, etc.

The twelve–step program is fundamentally based on ancient spiritual principles and rooted in sound medical therapy. The best recommendation for the program is the fact that "it works."

Training–Wheel Prayer for Food Addiction by Liberty Savard[43]

"I bind my body, soul, and spirit to your will, confessing that I know I don't do what's best for me to do. I bind my attitudes about eating, my stubborn emotions, and my mind's desires to eat when I'm bored, all to your will. I bind my soul and its desire (to stuff my body and dull my senses when it is responding to reactivated pain) to your will. I want and need to have my soul brought under the control of your will, Father! I loose the self–justification, self–desire, self–deception, and the self–denial that I have allowed my soul to layer over my unmet needs. Forgive me, Lord, for using food to try to take the edge off the driving force of these needs. In Jesus' name, amen."

Resources

Teen Challenge has faith–based residential treatment programs to help men and women of all ages to overcome substance abuse and become established as Christians. www.teenchallenge.com

http://www.kadd.org/Self%20Tests.htm offers a self–test to determine if you are an addict.

www.alcoholicsforchrist.com

www.settingcaptivesfree.com—free alcohol, overeating, same–sex attraction and pornography/masturbation online courses with an assigned mentor. Also provides the "Pure Freedom Mentor's Guide" if you want to lead a group for men addicted to porn. (also available at www.christianbook.com)

http://www.christians–in–recovery.org/resources/tools/toolkit.html—has a toolkit, a life recovery Bible and a recovery devotional Bible companion for 12 step recovery.

www.alcoholics–anonymous.org

Overeaters Anonymous—www.oa.org

Sex and Love Addicts Anonymous www.sexaa.org

Books

Way of Escape—Neil T. Anderson

Addicted to Love—Stephen Arterburn

The Sexual Addiction—Patrick Carnes

We Are Driven—Robert Hemfelt, Frank Minirth, and Paul Meier

101 Freedom Exercises: Christian Guide for Sex Addiction Recovery—Douglas Weiss and Dianne DeBusk

Women Who Love Sex Addicts—Douglas Weiss and Dianne DeBusk

Freedom from Addiction—Neil T. Anderson

Freedom from Addiction Workbook—Neil T. Anderson

Overcomers Outreach: A Bridge to Recovery— Bob Bartosch and Pauline Bartosch

I'll Quit Tommorow—Vernon Johnson

Counselling for Substance Abuse and Addiction—Stephen Van Cleave, Walter Byrd, and Kathy Revell

OVERCOMING ANXIETY

According to the National Institute of Mental Health, more than 23 million people suffer from anxiety disorders. Christians are no exception. Anxiety has many roots. You may experience anxiety if you feel threatened in any way (your personal safety, self–esteem, relationships with others) or when dealing with conflicts. You may also experience anxiety when confronted with an underlying fear such as failure, rejection, the future, finances, health, and so forth.

The Greek word for anxiety in the Bible is from two root words, meaning divide and mind. "A double–minded man is unstable in all he does" (James 1:8). Paul urged us "not to be anxious about anything, in everything, by prayer and petition, with thanksgiving, present your requests to God" (Philippians 4:6). Jesus Himself said, "Let not your heart be troubled" (John 14:1). Notice He said "let not," meaning you have a choice and can choose to look to God for strength and courage according to His promises and to not be afraid.

Steps to Overcome Anxiety

To overcome anxiety, you need to correct irrational thinking with reality, improve your coping strategies, increase your self–esteem, encourage appropriate risk taking, identify effective solutions to anxiety, and practice positive self–talk.

You first need to become aware of how it affects you physically. Are your muscles tense? Is your heart pounding? Are your hands cold and clammy? Experiment with different techniques to see what works for you to calm yourself such as: breathing exercises, stretching exercises, biofeedback, meditation on the Word of God, massage, visual imagery, or progressive muscle relaxation.

Once you know how your body responds to stress/anxiety acquaint yourself with the people, things, and events that are triggering your stress. Avoiding stressors is one option and learning to manage them realistically is another. You need to maintain balance and perspective in your life; you want to achieve a sense of perceived control.

Regular physical exercise helps reduce stress, increases self–esteem, and it does not need to be rigorous. Walking at a brisk pace for twenty or thirty minutes daily decreases stress just as effectively as jogging. Find things to do that you enjoy: listening to music, prayer, sports, dance, painting, nature walks, writing—whatever helps to relax you or make you feel refreshed.

Much stress, especially these days, comes from taking on too much at once. It may help to re–evaluate what is really important in our lives so we give our time more completely to the things that matter the most. Bringing expectations into line with reality and learning to say no when we choose to are also effective for reducing stress. In relationships, learn to express your needs without being aggressive or being taken advantage of in your dealings with other people.

Develop a good support system; surround yourself with people who can nurture and support you. A friend may act as a "sounding board" and can help us to put things into a more realistic perspective and just being able to express ourselves serves to reduce our stress levels.

Test reality. Separate facts from assumptions. Some people are afraid of things like being hit by lightning when the odds of that actually happening are astronomical. Make a list of what you have the ability to control and take responsibility for those things. For example, if you have a heart attack, you may not be able to control when you might have another one but you can improve your lifestyle and diet.

It is important to be in a right relationship with God to overcome anxiety. James 4:7 admonishes us to submit ourselves to God, that "if we resist the devil, he will flee from us. But notice the condition—if we are submitted to God, so resolve all known personal and spiritual conflicts in your life.

When you pray, ask God to show you things from His perspective—sometimes a different slant on things changes our outlook so that things appear more manageable. Claim Bible verses that are particularly helpful for you personally.

The rest is God's responsibility—commit it to Him. Some people find it helpful to visualize handing their problems over to God. For example, imagine a small hot air balloon with your problem written on a piece of paper in the balloon and then see it floating up to the heavens as you release it to God. This can be a good exercise to do before going to sleep.

When you are stressed out about something, like just before going into a job interview or having to do a public presentation, take a few moments to close your eyes and imagine yourself on a beach relaxing in the sun while you do some deep breathing for a few minutes.

Remind yourself of God's love and care (Matthew 6:25–32). Ask yourself if you are putting Him first in your life. Matthew 6:33 reminds us to "seek the Kingdom of God first and His righteousness and then all these things shall be added unto you." Think of being in a boat; if you only have today's worries with you in the boat, you will float, but if you add yesterday's troubles and tomorrow's anxiety, you will sink. Live one day at a time. One of my favourite verses is Jeremiah 29:11, "For I know the thoughts that I think toward you, saith the Lord, thoughts of peace, and not of evil, to give you an expected end."

We are free from the anxiety of guilt because of Jesus' sacrifice on the cross. He intercedes as our High Priest (Hebrews 4:14) providing peace for us. He reigns as King of kings and Lord of lords; He is in control of everything and we are in His hands! "He will never leave us or abandon us" (Matthew 28:20).

Change your thinking to reflect Jesus' teachings. In John 16:13 Jesus reminds us, "These things I have spoken unto you, that in me ye might have peace. In the world ye shall have tribulation: but be of good cheer; I have overcome the world."

If you have already tried most of the above, sometimes medication can be useful for relieving symptoms of anxiety. They include antidepressants and are usually administered through trial and error to see which medications and dosage are beneficial to a particular patient. The problem with medication, however, is that it can only relieve symptoms and does not deal with the root causes of anxiety.

The behavioural therapy approach attempts to change actions through relaxation techniques or through gradual exposure to the source of anxiety that also focuses on the symptoms.

Cognitive therapy is more about retraining your thinking so you can respond differently to situations that cause anxiety and it also addresses the underlying causes. As Christians, we can take cognitive therapy one step further. When we examine the underlying fear thoughts, we can apply biblical responses. Worry can be countered with Philippians 4:19 where we have God's promise to take care of all our needs and in 1 Peter 5:7 we are encouraged us to cast all our anxieties on Jesus who cares for us.

Think about something you are anxious or worried about right now in your life. Now, ask yourself what is the worst thing that could happen to you because of this? Then tell yourself that even if it actually happened to you (most of the things we worry about do *not* happen to us) that you would survive, that God would help you cope with it, you could learn from it and move on. Believe that "all things work together for good" (Romans 8:28) and that "He has made everything beautiful in His time" (Ecclesiastes 3:11) and that "no weapon formed against you shall prosper" (Isaiah 54:17).

Self–Care

Plan things as much as possible to give yourself a sense of control and accept responsibility for your health and well–being. Remember to take time out for you:

- Listen to relaxing music.

- Have a hot bath with candles glowing all around the tub.

- Write notes in a journal for insight into what stressors affect you the most and what is most helpful for you in counteracting stress.

- Limit smoking and alcohol use. (Preferably cease smoking or the causes of stress without eliminating them. Alcohol intake disturbs regular sleep patterns and disguises symptoms.)

- Maintain a balanced diet as much as possible, ensure you are getting enough sleep and exercise.

- Use positive self-talk "I can handle this" or "It's okay—I can do this."

- Change what you can, accept what you cannot.

- Maintain a good support system; don't neglect opportunities to talk with friends.

- Laugh—it may boost the immune system and lower stress levels.

- Clarify family member's roles and responsibilities.

- Make the time for quiet reflection.

- Pray. If you are concerned about something that is not in your control, give it up to God. Otherwise, ask God how He would have you handle it and let go of the anxiety.

- Praise.

- Say no to any activities that won't fit into your schedule or that will cause you more stress.
- Delegate responsibilities to others if possible.
- Prepare a monthly budget and stick to it.
- Memorize and write out your favourite Bible verses to refer to often.
- Maintain "an attitude of gratitude."
- Nurse no grudges, hold no resentment toward anyone.
- Slow down.

If the above suggestions are not effective, or if you believe you are suffering from severe anxiety, talk to your doctor or seek the help of a counsellor. It is a strength, not a weakness, to recognize your limits and seek support when needed.

Generalized Anxiety Disorder is when one exhibits an anxiety trait most days for a six month period such as: being excessively worried, being on edge continually, having sleep difficulty, and finding it hard to experience pleasure and relaxation. The intensity of the worry is out of proportion to the cause.

Post–Traumatic Stress Disorder (PTSD) may be the result of experiencing a serious, life–threatening event, and one can suffer long–term effects such as: nightmares, hypervigilance, and avoiding similar situations.

Obsessive–Compulsive Disorder (OCD) may occur when stress or chaos in one's world causes a person to think and worry repetitively about something. Compulsive thoughts are called obsessions and repetitive behaviours like hand washing or checking on things excessively are called compulsions.

Christians are not immune to Generalized Anxiety Disorder, PTSD, or OCD, and some Christians experience dramatic episodes of stress that seem to appear suddenly, which are known as *panic attacks*. They are usually intense with symptoms of chest pains, the feeling of smothering, dizziness, heart pounding, sweating, numbness, or nausea. Fears of dying, going crazy, and losing control may accompany the physical symptoms. Those who experience panic attacks often dread their next attack to the point where they may not leave their home or drive in their car.

One of the best ways to manage a panic attack is to just let it happen, as uncomfortable as this may seem. If you don't tense up physically, the symptoms will probably subside within a few minutes. You may feel faint because your blood pressure and heart rate have increased, but you won't really faint. During a panic attack, challenge your negative thinking and practice self–calming positive talk such as, "I am not having a heart attack," " I will not suffocate," "I am not going crazy," and then follow it with a verse like, "God has not given me a spirit of fear, but of love and power and a sound mind" (2 Timothy 1:7). Assure yourself that it will and momentarily pass and say things like, "Let me watch my body respond to this, just like I've done before. God is with me and I will survive this. It is only anxiety and it will pass."

If you think you may be experiencing symptoms of PTSD, OCD, or panic attacks, again, you should consult with your physician or Christian psychiatrist as they can both prescribe medication (if necessary) and see a pastor with training in counselling or a Christian therapist.

Prayer

Father, I cast my cares (name them), all my anxieties, worries, concerns, once and for all on You. I cast down imaginations and every high thing that exalts itself against the knowledge of You and I bring every thought into obedience to Christ. I lay aside every weight that tries to beset me. I will not let my heart be troubled and I will focus on those things that are lovely, of a good report, virtuous, and worthy of praise. I declare that I walk in the peace that passes all understanding, in Jesus' name.

Resources:

Freedom from Fear—Neil T. Anderson

Healing Fear—Edmund J. Bourne

Feel the Fear and Do It Anyway—Susan Jeffers

Don't Panic—Reid R. Wilson

A Layman's Guide to Managing Fear Using Psychology, Christianity, and Non Resistant Methods, at http://www. trebleheartbooks.com/mvStanPopovich.html

http://www.ncptsd.va.gov/facts/specific/index.html National Center for PTSD (US Dept. of Veteran Affairs)

www.panic–anxiety.com

support@panic–anxiety.com

OVERCOMING DEPRESSION

If you are a Christian who suffers from depression, you are not alone. Great men of God have been known to suffer depression including Elijah, David, and Jeremiah. Depressive disorders affect approximately 18.8 million American adults or about 9.5% of the U.S. population.[44] Depression will be the second largest killer after heart disease by 2020 and studies show depression is a contributory factor to fatal coronary disease. [45]

Symptoms of Depression[46]

- Abnormal depressed mood (feeling hopeless, discouraged)
- Abnormal loss of all interest and pleasure
- Appetite or weight disturbance
- Abnormal sleep: difficulty falling asleep, frequent awakenings during the night or very early morning awakening. Excessive sleeping is a less common symptom.
- Abnormal fatigue or loss of energy
- Abnormal self–reproach or inappropriate guilt, significant reduction of self–esteem and self–confidence with increased thoughts of pessimism, hopelessness, and helplessness
- Abnormal poor concentration or indecisiveness

If you have experienced several of the above symptoms for more than a period of two weeks and it is a change from your usual functioning, you should ask your family physician to assess you for clinical depression. You may be having a major depressive episode.

You may have heard the term bi–polar disorder, formerly known as manic depression. I think there are a lot of misconceptions about bipolar disorder, which involves experiencing alternating periods of mania with depression. Manic behaviour includes: inflated self–esteem or grandiosity, being unusually talkative, racing thoughts, distractibility, and excessive involvement in pleasurable activities that have a high potential for painful consequences, such as unrestrained buying sprees, sexual indiscretions, foolish business investments, etc.[47] Lithium is often prescribed to stabilize moods.

Causes

Short–term depression may be caused by a recent loss or trauma. This is more of a "reactive" depression. Chronic or long–term depression may be caused by trauma in childhood, which includes: emotional, physical or sexual abuse, neglect, maternal separation, conflict in the family, violence in the family, racism, and poverty. [48]

There may be a genetic basis to some depression, but even then, researchers from Harvard and Johns Hopkins universities assert that genetic propensity must be triggered by some traumatic or stressful event.[49] Recent studies indicate that serotonin, which is targeted by most anti-depressants, is not as much a factor in depression as the long–term presence of stress hormone cortisol.[50]

Your doctor can rule out any physiological causes such as anemia, hypothyroidism, chronic infection, substance abuse, neurological disorders, multiple sclerosis, Parkinson's disease, migraine, various forms of epilepsy, encephalitis, brain tumors, diabetes, strokes, and so forth.

Many medications can cause depression, especially blood pressure medications such as calcium channel blockers, beta blockers, analgesics, and some anti–migraine medications and oral contraceptives.

Some people may experience depression as a result of guilt over past sins; however, to not accept God's forgiveness is to leave Jesus on the cross. He already paid the price and to not forgive yourself is tantamount to saying that Jesus' sacrifice was not good enough for you.

"If the Son therefore shall make you free, ye shall be free indeed"(John 8:36).

Some Christians may experience depression as a result of generational curses or involvement in occult–related practices, unconfessed sin, etc. See the chapter on "Seven Steps to Spiritual Freedom" and read Neil Anderson's book *Steps to Freedom* to ensure that there are no spiritual causes for your depression.

Treatment for Depression

Medication

Most anti–depressants affect the serotonin levels in the brain. Antidepressants are effective for 35 to 45% of the depressed population, while more recent figures suggest as low as 30%.

[51]Standard antidepressants such as Prozac, Paxil, and Zoloft have recently been revealed to have serious risks and are linked to suicide, violence, psychosis, abnormal bleeding, and brain tumors. [52]

If you do use anti–depressant medication, be sure to see your doctor on a regular basis to monitor the drug and the dosage. Another option may be to try herbal supplements such as St. John's Wort. Most physicians recommend a combination of anti–depressants and supportive therapy. Recovery from depression with long–term results requires addressing the underlying causes of depression.

Cognitive therapy seems to be most effective. If you are depressed it could be due to negative thinking patterns related to your outlook on yourself, your life, and your future. If you would like to understand more about cognitive therapy, read *Feeling Good: The New Mood Therapy* by Dr. David Burns (1980, revised 1999) in which Burns identifies twelve specific negative thinking patterns.

Any negative thinking pattern can be superimposed with a new positive thinking pattern like re–wallpapering the room of your mind. The first thing to do is make a habit of catching yourself thinking something negative and then nip those thoughts in the bud by replacing those thoughts immediately with positive, affirming statements and then quoting a scripture verse to reinforce it as truth.

For example, you do poorly on a test or exam of some sort and you catch yourself thinking, *I am a failure. I am never going to get ahead.* You then instantly replace that line of thinking by recalling some examples of being successful, no matter how trivial. Then encourage yourself by saying things like, "Even though I failed that test, I am a competent person and my worth is not dependent on any external performance. I am learning and I will improve. I will study/practice harder and pass the test next time." Then quote a Bible verse like, "I can do all things through Christ who strengthens me" (Philippians 4:13).

Of course, in order for this to be effective, it takes consistent practice. You haven't developed negative thinking patterns overnight and it will take effort over time to make positive thinking based on the Word of God part of your "automatic" thinking process. The biblical principle of renewing your mind (Romans 12:2) is an effective form of cognitive therapy for Christians. We can combat negative thinking patterns with the truth from the Word of God.

"Brethren, whatsoever things are true, whatsoever things are honest, whatsoever things are just, whatsoever things are pure, whatsoever things are lovely, whatsoever things are of good report; if there be any virtue, and if there be any praise, think on these things" (Philippians 4:8).

How to Reframe the Past

Out of adversity comes strength, or, as the Stewart Clan motto purports, "Courage gains strength from a wound." As we begin to make sense of past hurts we can minimize their effects. You have a choice: you can dwell on the past, which reinforces all the negativity associated with it, or you can change your self–talk and what you say to others about it.

Try to find value in having experienced traumatic circumstances. Ask yourself, How can those experiences make me a stronger or wiser person? A better Christian? A better witness? More compassionate? More tolerant? More thankful? We cannot undo the past and when we constantly talk about the past trauma, we reinforce its influence on us in the present. There is healing in being able to change destructive, toxic thoughts to positive, nurturing thoughts.

When you begin to be aware of upsetting painful memories, immediately take control of your reaction and reframe the pain—stop the pattern by mentally saying to yourself, with conviction, "I choose to let go of my suffering." Then immediately recall a memory of a loving, happy experience of the past. Some people actually find it difficult to "let go" of suffering only because it is familiar, almost like an old shoe or an old friend. New, unknown territory is scary and not as appealing even though it may be far more healthy.

There is great peace in accepting your current circumstances and in accepting the past for what it was. "The one thing I do, however, is to forget what is behind me and do my best to reach what is ahead" (Philippians 3:13). Acceptance helps to release you from the pain of the past. You accumulated pain along your life's journey but you now have the awareness and the ability to leave it in the past and move forward. Choose healing now. Commit your past to God and let it go once and for all.

Now, add gratitude to acceptance. We need to appreciate the blessings we have been given and we need to learn to focus on those blessings. Put a positive spin on whatever life offers you, and receive it thankfully knowing that there is something to be achieved even from trials and pain.

1 Thessalonians 5: 16–18 reminds us of this with, "Be joyful always, pray at all times, be thankful in all circumstances. This is what God wants from you in your life in union with Christ Jesus." James 1:2 continues to encourage us with, "Consider yourself fortunate when all kinds of trials come your way for you know that when your faith succeeds in facing such trials, the result is the ability to endure."

Your pain may draw you nearer to God and mistakes you regret may have taught you lessons otherwise never learned. Looking for the gain in the pain can promote personal growth. Pray and ask God what He is trying to teach you by allowing those difficult circumstances.

A spiritual perspective enables you to stand back and see that the pain of the past is a very small part of our eternal destiny. No matter what or how long we have suffered, when we look at the "big picture," it helps reframe the significance of our suffering in the past. Think of a sentence that has a few words in brackets, that is like our life in the context of eternity. Pray that you will come to understand the depths, height, and breadth of God's love for you. In heaven you will feel the way you always wanted to feel, you will get whatever you need there that you might not be able to have here. The best really is yet to come.

Interpersonal therapy and communication skills can help you deal more effectively with other people, which will improve your relationships, therefore, reducing depression. Reconcile with God and others if there is any resentment in your heart.

A good support system is essential. Christians should be able to connect with other Christians for support by participating in small groups at their local church or by attending Alpha Groups (www.alphana.org) if they are lacking support from family members. Our church family should provide strength, patience, and encouragement to those who are depressed. Remember, we are to bear one another's burdens (Galatians 6:–2, 1 Thessalonians 5:14). Create relationships that meet needs not met in childhood, including looking to God to meet your emotional needs and for inner healing.

Do you have a pet? Researchers have found petting an animal can help fight depression. Interaction with pets reduces stress by lowering cortisol levels and reduces depression by increasing serotonin levels in the brain.[53]

Death Wishes

If a child experiences trauma, rejection, or a lot of negative emotion while in the womb, the child's response is that the world is not a friendly place and they don't want to be in it. They may unconsciously assume a "death wish," which, if not dealt with, may result in physical illnesses and depression and suicidal thoughts for years or throughout their entire life, even in a spirit–filled Christian.[54]

To determine if you or someone you know has a death wish, ask questions such as:

- If you were in heaven with Jesus and He asked you to volunteer to go to earth, how would you feel about that?

- Would you choose to be born to your parents? In another time or place?

- Do you like yourself including your face, body, and mind?

- If Jesus gave you a choice to go to heaven right now or live out your life on earth however many years that may entail, what would your response be?

If a person would rather not be here in all honesty, they are actually admitting that they are angry with God for putting them here in their circumstances and they are unhappy with what God created them to be. In order to reconcile with God, then, one has to choose to accept being what God created him or her to be and repent for rejecting their life on earth and to choose to join Jesus in accepting themselves as they are in every moment of their life.

If you are praying for someone with a death wish or for yourself, after repenting for rejecting God for creating who they or who you are in their circumstances, ask Jesus to minister to their inner child, for an integration and harmony of spirit, heart, mind, and body, and take authority in Jesus' name to break any inner vows wishing death. Ask the person to say "I choose life" out loud on a daily basis until they feel they believe it deep down inside of them.

Suicide

Job wished he had never been born, David had bouts of severe depression, Jonah asked God to kill him in Jonah 4:3, and Elijah as well. We can understand their reactions to their circumstances; however, I have to wonder if they were full of self–pity, self–righteousness, and not yielding personal rights to God, or if they were clinically depressed.

Jonah, for example, was angry because God did not do things as Jonah expected. He did not accept God's sovereignty and He discounted all the things God did to minister to him. God spoke to Jonah, prepared the fish to save him, answered his prayers to escape the great fish, He tried to reason with Jonah and prepared a gourd for him, etc. Jonah was focused on his own perspective of fairness. He thought he had a right to be angry and a right to the shade of the gourd and so forth. In his case, it seems as though he needed to let God be God and not insist that his personal rights be met, and yet, how patient God was with him. But imagine how things would have turned out if these men had actually taken their own lives. What a tragedy that would have been! What a waste of ministry potential!

I am reminded of a true story of a nineteen-year–old young man who killed himself because he thought he had failed his university exams. Higher education was an important value to his parents and he felt he had let them down. As it turned out, he passed his exams after all; however, even if he hadn't, he could have re–written them or chosen a different career or gotten counselling to deal with his parents' expectations and increased his self–esteem. There are always options and suicide is never the answer.

According to the Agency for Healthcare Research and Quality (2003), 15% of depressed people will commit suicide. An astounding total of 31,655 individuals completed suicide in 2002—one person approximately every 17.2 minutes.[55] Of those 31,655 individuals, approximately 4,010 were youth between fifteen and twenty–four years old. Suicide is the eleventh leading cause of death in the United States; however, it is the third leading cause of death for youth (ages 15–24), exceeded only by accidents and homicides. Annually, 790,000 Americans have attempted to kill themselves.

People contemplating suicide don't really wish to die. For whatever reason, they are in unbearable pain or anguish and they just want to put an end to their suffering. Risk factors are stressful events or conditions that increase the likelihood that one will attempt/complete suicide.

Risk factors may include any of the following:

- Previous suicide attempt(s)
- Depression
- Combined mental health and substance abuse issues
- Hopelessness/Helplessness
- Loss (relationships, health, identity status)
- Exposure to suicide (family, peers, significant others)
- Physical, emotional, and sexual abuse
- Gender identity conflict

Warning signs may be someone giving away possessions or putting their affairs in order, a radical shift in characteristic behaviour: withdrawal; anxiety; changed social habits; a pervasive feeling of hopelessness/helplessness; being preoccupied; troubled by past physical, emotional, or sexual abuse; exhibiting a profound degree of one or more emotions such as anger, loneliness, guilt, hostility, or grief. Verbal/written clues may be statements such as, "I'm of no use to anyone anymore" to "This time I am going to kill myself." Behavioural clues could be superficial slashing of the wrist and situational clues may be concern over illness, finances, preoccupation with a loved one's death.

One way to assess if a person is seriously planning to take his own life is if he has a detailed plan of how he would do it and if he has the means to do it. Vague statements such as, "I'm so tired, what's the use?" or, "Things would be better if I wasn't even here," are cues but if a person states specifics such as he is going to hang himself Tuesday afternoon and he already has the rope, for example, he needs to be hospitalized immediately.

Treatment

If you suspect someone you know is suicidal or he says that he is, refer him to professional help immediately, even if you have to break confidentiality, and then stay with him or make sure someone else stays with him until he is under professional care.

Try to convince him that he can feel better, impart hope, tell him things can be different. Help him to separate thoughts from action, get him to sign a "no–harm contract" with you, explore alternatives to his problems, and provide referral resources.

Ask him what would want to make him continue living and try to get him to promise he won't hurt himself while you figure out some options together. Ask him how relatives would feel and pray with him. Try saying anything you can think of that will help a person change his mind about committing suicide. I have even brought up heaven and hell and if he has considered spending eternity in pain as opposed to temporary pain on earth. Suicide is a permanent solution to a temporary problem.

Then ask him which of the options you have discussed seem best to him. Try to get him to commit to an alternate plan of action. Ask who can help support him at this time. Take him to the nearest emergency department if you cannot ensure that someone will be with him even if he has said he has abandoned his plan to commit suicide.

If you are reading this and you are suicidal, please call 1–800–suicide (784–2433) or your doctor or clergyperson now. Online you can speak to someone in real time chat at www.samaritans.org or www.newhopenow.org. Tell someone how you are feeling and know that you can feel better, circumstances can improve, and you are not alone. God is with you and loves you and others do too. The pain you are feeling will not last forever.

Prayer for Overcoming Depression[56]

"Father, You are my refuge and my high tower and my stronghold in times of trouble. I lean on and confidently put my trust in You, for You have not forsaken me. I seek You on the authority of Your Word and the right of my necessity. I praise You, the help of my countenance and my God.

Lord, You lift up those who are bowed down. Therefore I am strong and my heart takes courage. I establish myself on righteousness, right standing in conformity with Your will and order. I am far even from the thought of oppression or destruction, for I fear not. I am far from terror, for it shall not come near me.

Father, You have thoughts and plans for my welfare and peace. My mind is stayed on You, for I stop allowing myself to be agitated and disturbed and intimidated and cowardly and unsettled.

Satan, I resist you and every oppressive spirit in the name of Jesus. I resist fear, discouragement, self–pity, and depression. I speak the Word of truth, in the power of God, and I give you no place, Satan; I give no opportunity to you. I am delivered from oppression by the blood of the Lamb.

Father, I thank You that I have been given a spirit of power and love and of a calm and well–balanced mind. I have discipline and self–control. I have the mind of Christ and hold the thoughts, feelings, and purpose of His heart. I have a fresh mental and spiritual attitude, for I am constantly renewed in the spirit of my mind with Your Word, Father.

Therefore, I brace up and reinvigorate and cut through and make firm and straight paths for my feet, safe and upright and happy paths that go in the right direction. I arise from the depression and prostration in which circumstances have kept me. I rise to new life; I shine and am radiant with the glory of the Lord. Thank You, Father, in Jesus' name that I am set free from every evil work. I praise You that the joy of the Lord is my strength and stronghold! Hallelujah."

Scriptural Encouragement

The Lord is near to those who are discouraged, he saves those who have lost all hope.

Psalm 34:18

Fear thou not; for I am with thee: be not dismayed; for I am thy God: I will strengthen thee; yea, I will help thee; yea, I will uphold thee with the right hand of my righteousness.

Isaiah 41:10

As a shepherd carries a lamb, I have carried you close to my heart.

Isaiah 40:11

I am also the Father who comforts you in all your troubles.

2 Corinthians 1:3–4

One day I will wipe away every tear from your eyes.

Revelation 21:3–4

And I'll take away all the pain you have suffered on this earth.

Revelation 21:3–4

When thou passest through the waters, I will be with thee; and through the rivers, they shall not overflow thee: when thou walkest through the fire, thou shalt not be burned; neither shall the flame kindle upon thee.

Isaiah 43:2

He healeth the broken in heart, and bindeth up their wounds.

Psalms 147:3

The righteous cry, and the Lord heareth, and delivereth them out of all their troubles.

Psalms 34:17

And nothing will ever separate you from my love again.

Romans 8:38–39

Resources:

Finding Hope Again—Neil T. Anderson

Counselling the Depressed—Archibald Hart

Overcoming Depression—Demitiri Papolos and Janice Papolos

Guidebooks on depression to download: supporting your partner, managing depression, shared guidebook

http://www.supportpartnersprogram.com/guidebooks/guide-books.jsp

RELATIONSHIPS

Relationships are the most important thing in life. When we die God will not be interested in how much money we earned, how many degrees we had, or how far we got in our career, He will want to know how well we loved other people.

The majority of people seeking counseling with me are dealing with a difficult relationship issue, often a wife trying to figure out if there is any way she can or should stay in her marriage. I quote the usual verses from the Bible and let the person decide what to do based on what she believes God personally requires of her.

Most marriages are salvageable, even when infidelity has occurred. Each spouse should do everything in their power to save their marital relationship. Marriage is about meeting each other's needs, and in order to meet each other's needs, couples need to be able to effectively communicate their needs to each other. Fortunately, communication skills can be taught. If a couple is not able to improve their relationship on their own, they should seek professional or pastoral help. There are often older, spiritually mature couples in your church that may act as "couple mentors" as well, if the need is made known.

What general principles does the Bible give us about relationships?

Love is patient and kind, love is not jealous or boastful or proud or rude. Love does not demand its own way. Love is not irritable, and it keeps no record of when it has been wronged. It is never glad about injustice. Love never gives up, never loses faith, is always hopeful, and endures through every circumstance. Love will last forever.

I Corinthians 13:4–8a (New Living Bible)

Such agape love requires the husband to always put his wife's needs above his own and to give himself in self–sacrificial service to her. Paul tells the church in Ephesus to submit themselves mutually to one another (Ephesians 5:21). Then, beginning in Ephesians 5:22, he explains in some detail how that submission and a servant's heart are to be expressed within marriage.

In a *Portrait of Christ for Newlyweds,* we read:

Self–denial is chosen when marriage is chosen. For marriage is not a union to ease the burdens of life, but a selfless sharing of greater responsibilities. Continually marriage asks for self–denial and through this its deepest joys are won. For marriage soon shows us that true love is forever bound to self–denial, never counts the cost, and finds its reward in giving.

The best thing you can do for your mate is to become like Christ and then begin to treat your spouse as Christ would.

Emotional Intimacy

The happiest couples enjoy emotional intimacy in their relationship. What is emotional intimacy? It's about inviting someone to enter your private world. If a wife, in particular, doesn't feel like she has emotional intimacy with her husband, she will be unhappy in their relationship. Emotional intimacy is about communicating at deep levels with another person, sharing what you know about yourself with another person who can be trusted.

So, first off, you need a sense of commitment to and from that person. True intimacy is reserved for a person who will be there for you over the long haul, such as a close friend, a partner, a family member, or a spouse. You also need a sense of trust. If the other person is not able to appreciate you making yourself vulnerable to them, it is futile to try to achieve intimacy. In the worst scenario, your words might even be held against you later, which would be very damaging leading to distrust.

Creating intimacy means taking a risk, opening yourself up, sharing that which is the most personal part of yourself with another person so a guarded or defensive person will never achieve real intimacy with anyone. If the other person receives the sharing of yourself, it is a precious gift to you and to your relationship. If they handle it with care, then you are no longer alone in the world.

Intimacy has to be reciprocal. There can be no power differential if true emotional intimacy is to be developed and maintained. The receiver of private and delicate information has to be able to honour and respect the openness, vulnerability, and courage of the one who is giving of themselves by sharing very personal ideas and emotions. This is not the time for value judgments, criticisms, and/or advice giving. The objective is to appreciate and to validate the deepest feelings of the other person.

If you are lacking emotional intimacy with your partner, there are ways to develop the kind of emotional connection that promotes trust and mutual consideration. Aside from personal sharing, it would be a good idea to get a babysitter and spend one night a week out together as a couple to do the activities you enjoy doing together and to have a chance to reconnect with each other as a "couple." Praying together is another good way to develop emotional intimacy as well as spiritual intimacy.

Commitment

Ask yourself where you would rate yourself in terms of commitment to your relationship on a scale of 1–10 (if 1 is you are ready for a divorce and 10 is you will do anything to save your relationship/marriage). Then, whatever your score, ask yourself what it would take to get your commitment level to a 10 and start those steps based on what *you* can change. Love is choice—a decision. The following story by Dr. Neil Clark Warren[57] will give you some idea of how much the will is involved in a relationship.

A man went to his attorney and announced that he was ready for a divorce. He no longer found his wife attractive. She was caustic, overweight, and frumpy. The two were at war, fighting constantly and he had grown to hate her. The attorney listened for a while and then offered the following suggestion. "I can hear how much you detest this woman and I have a plan to inflict maximum damage on her. Go home and spend the next thirty days treating her like the most important person in the world. Engage her in conversation and listen attentively. Help her around the house. Take her to dinner, and see a romantic movie once a week. Do everything in your power to be kind to her. You will have set her up for the biggest hurt of her life. *Then* we will serve her with the divorce papers and she will be devastated. I'll have the papers ready in thirty days."

The husband was more than happy to carry out the vicious setup. He went home and immediately began to practice all the unscrupulous suggestions that the lawyer had given him. Thirty days later the attorney called the man to tell him that the papers were ready to be served. But the husband was horrified at the very suggestion of divorce. "Divorce?" he said. "Why would I want to divorce her? She's an incredible woman, even better than when I first fell in love with her. She is everything I dreamed of. Why would I want to divorce her?"

It is a corny story. But the point is clear: certain actions create results. By taking concrete steps to engender passion and romance, you keep that flame alive throughout the years of your marriage—if you act as though you love someone, the feelings will come.

If you want to restore the magic in marriage, start behaving the way you did when you fell in love in the first place. Commitment is the foundation to marriage happiness and even if one person in the relationship is less motivated than you are to improve it, you can start a chain reaction of new interaction patterns with your spouse by first changing the way you act and react. Make a list of the reasons you should be fully committed to your marriage and then make another list of the ways in which your will begin demonstrating that commitment to your partner.

Dr. Pete Bruno[58] suggests the two of you make these affirmations of commitment to each other:

1. I am completely committed to my mate.
2. I am committed to good communication.
3. I am committed to be faithful and best friends.
4. I am committed to find resolutions for conflicts.
5. I am committed to share in interests and goals.
6. I am committed to provide sexual satisfaction.
7. I am committed to behave in financially secure ways.
8. I am committed to attend church together regularly.
9. I am committed to pray together daily.

Communication

It is vital to any healthy relationship to be able to communicate and to resolve conflicts. In order to meet each other's needs, you need to be able to clearly articulate to each other what your needs are and how to meet them exactly. Don't let things fester but before you approach your spouse, think about what you are going to say and couch it in "I" statements so that you don't come across as accusatory.

For example, your husband doesn't come home for dinner and doesn't call. When he finally arrives or calls, you can immediately let out all your frustration and browbeat him for not calling *or* you can calmly state something like, "You know, when you are late and you don't call, I get worried because I don't know what's happened to you." That way you are saying that *you* have a need to know that he is safe, which won't put him on the defensive.

If you are unhappy with a particular behaviour your spouse is exhibiting, first ask yourself why it bothers you. Could it be they remind you of someone else? Could it be that it triggers something negative from your childhood? Do you need to change your reaction instead?

If you can, pray together before having a discussion with your spouse, asking for God's wisdom and guidance. Then, be sure to validate each other's feelings and be specific about changes you are requesting. For example, "I want you to be more affectionate" is too vague so you need to say something like, "I would like you to be more affectionate. Can we cuddle on the couch or could you hold my hand sometimes or put your arm around me?"

Instead of thinking that you have a problem with your mate or your mate has a problem with you, try thinking of it as the two of you have a "relationship" problem that you can work on together to resolve. Always look for win–win solutions. Brainstorm together and settle on a solution you can both live with. You might want to do a "trade–off" sometimes. The husband will do/not do something to the please his wife and she will do/not do something in return to please him.

Be willing to ask yourself if you have contributed to the problem in any way. Review unsuccessful past attempts to solve the problem and try a new approach. Some believe that the definition of true love is doing everything they can to make their spouse happy without expecting anything in return. Make a list of the ways that you can be your mate's best friend.

Choose to be happy instead of being right. You don't have to prove that you know what you're talking about more than your partner. Instead, choose tolerance. Things will only get worse if you are being critical and negative, expecting your spouse to change first, or you are rejecting spouse's advances, blaming your spouse for the problem (except in abuse cases). Instead, work on promoting your partner's self-esteem.

Prayer by Holley Gerth[59]

Lord,
Because love is patient…
Help me to be slow to judge, but quick to listen.
Hesitant to criticize, but eager to encourage,
remembering your endless patience with me.

Because love is kind…
Help my words to be gentle and my actions to be thoughtful.
Remind me to smile and to say "Please" and "Thank You"
because those little things still mean so much.

Because love does not envy or boast, and it is not proud…
Help me have a heart that is humble and sees the good in others. May I celebrate and appreciate all that I have and all that I am, as well as doing the same for those around me.

Because love is not rude or self-seeking…
Help me to speak words that are easy on the ear and on the heart. When I'm tempted to get wrapped up in my own little world, remind me there's a great big world out there full of needs and hurts.

Because love is not easily angered and keeps no record of wrongs...
Help me to forgive others as you have forgiven me. When I want to hold onto a grudge, gently help me release it so I can reach out with a hand of love instead.

Because love does not delight in evil but rejoices with the truth...
Help me stand up for what is right and good. May I defend the defenseless, and help the helpless. Show me how I can make a difference.
Because love always protects and always trusts...
Help me to be a refuge for those around me. When the world outside is harsh and cold, may my heart be a place of acceptance and warmth.

Finally, because love always perseveres...
Help my heart continually beat with love for You and others. Thank you for this day when we celebrate love, and for showing us what that word really means. Amen.

Creating Spiritual Intimacy

Praying together regularly unites your hearts together with each other and God at the same time. "And a threefold cord is not quickly broken" (Ecclesiastes 4:12). Pray for each other's needs, whether they are physical, emotional, or spiritual.

Studying the Word of God together also promotes spiritual intimacy. You can do individual studies and then share what you learned with each other or you can use a Bible study guide and work on the same study together sharing answers with each other. Most Christian bookstores have many Bible study guides—see if you can find one for married couples.

You will also strengthen your spiritual bond if you are involved in some kind of ministry to others together. Perhaps you could lead a group together in your home or pray together for others or mentor a new Christian.

Abuse in Relationships

Abuse can take many forms—physical, emotional, psychological, verbal, and financial. Yelling, demeaning comments, name calling, rejection, ignoring, isolating, terrorizing, withholding physical/verbal affection, unreasonable demands, emotional blackmail, blaming, intimidation, use of fear, mockery, and threats are all examples of emotional and psychological abuse. If endured long enough, such abuse may result in eating disorders, unresolved health issues, sleep disorders, anxiety, panic attacks, fear, anger, hostility, guilt, shame, powerlessness, depression, low self–esteem, loss of trust, and withdrawal.

I do not believe that abuse glorifies God and I think that sometimes people value the institution of marriage more than they value the people in the marriage. Obviously, if someone is being physically abused by their partner or if their partner is physically abusing their children, they need to go to a safe place like a women's shelter immediately. Such abuse should not be tolerated and usually worsens as time goes on.

The Bible clearly teaches that wife is to submit herself to the authority of her husband (Ephesians 5:22; Titus 2:5; Colossians 3:18; I Peter 3:1). Wives are to be submissive to their husbands except if he asks her to sin, such as in viewing pornography or having an abortion, for example. In those cases, she needs to obey the higher authority—God. It is a sin for anyone to scream, cuss, shove, or hit anyone else, and this applies to husbands and wives. In fact, it is illegal for a husband to assault his wife in any way. If a wife cannot convince her husband that he is sinning according to the Word of God, she should follow the steps of church discipline as outlined in Matthew 18:15–18 and if necessary call the police based on Romans 13:1, "Let every soul be subject unto the higher powers. For there is no power but of God: the powers that be are ordained of God." Even if the husband is not a Christian, he is subject to the law of the land.

In the case of abusive partners, I suggest that the abusive spouse gets counseling and/or takes anger management courses, and that the couple goes for relationship counseling while they are separated. It is better if the abused spouse does not reconcile to living together with the abusive spouse until that person has consistently demonstrated over a long period of time that they have genuinely changed their attitudes and behaviour.

For borderline cases only, where the husband may be somewhat abusive but the woman has been able to tolerate less than ideal behaviour, I ask the person to really seek God's will in the matter. Some women may be asked by God to endure an unpleasant marriage for a time because God knows her husband may get saved or that he will change in the future. Sometimes, God may want someone to stay in a miserable (but not significantly abusive) relationship for a time because God wants to shape their character and make them more Christlike.

Warning Signs of An Abusive Partner[60]
Jealousy

Jealousy has nothing to do with love; it's a sign of possessiveness and lack of trust. The abuser will question the victim about who he/she talks to, accusations of flirting are often heard, or the abuser may express resentment of time he/she spends with family, friends, or children. The abuser may call frequently or drop by unexpectedly. The abuser may refuse to let the victim work for fear he/she will meet someone else.

Controlling Behaviour

The abuser will be angry if the victim is "late" and will question whereabouts, who was seen or spoken to, etc. As this behaviour gets worse, the abuser may not allow the victim to make personal decisions about the house, for example, what clothes to wear, or decisions about going to church. An abuser may keep all of the money or even make the victim ask permission to leave the house or room.

Quick Involvement

An abuser may come on like a whirlwind, claiming, "You're the only person I could ever talk to," "I've never felt loved like this by anyone." The abuser may pressure a victim to commit to the relationship in such a way that brings about feelings of guilt if the victim wants to slow down involvement or break off the relationship at a later date.

Unrealistic Expectations

Abusive persons may expect the victims to meet all of their needs. The abuser may expect the man/woman to be the perfect husband/wife, father/mother, lover, friend, and will say things like, "If you love me, I'm all you need; you're all I need." The abuser may insist that the victim must be obedient in all things, including things that are criminal in nature.

Isolation

A victim may even be kept away from family members. The abuser may accuse friends and family of "causing trouble."

Blames Others for Problems

Someone is always doing him/her wrong. The abuser may make mistakes and then blame the victim for upsetting him/her.

Blames Others for Feelings

The abuser may tell the victim, "You make me so mad," "You're hurting me by not doing what I tell you," or, "I can't help being angry." The abuser makes the decision about what he/she feels, but will use feelings to manipulate the victim.

Hypersensitivity

An abuser is easily insulted. The abuser will rant and rave about the injustice of things that happen, things that are really just a part of life, such as being asked to work overtime, getting a traffic ticket, being told a behavior is annoying, or being asked to help with chores.

Cruelty to Children and Animals

The abuser may expect children to do things beyond their ability (e.g. spanks a two–year–old for wetting a diaper), or the abuser may tease children or young brothers and sisters until they cry. This is also a person who punishes animals brutally, is insensitive to their pain and suffering, or may even kill a victim's pet to hurt him/her.

"Playful" Use of Force in Sex

This kind of person may like to throw the victim down or hold them down during sex. The abuser may want to act out fantasies during sex where the victim is helpless and the idea of rape is exciting. The abuser may attempt having intercourse while the victim is sleeping or demand sex when he/she is ill or tired.

Verbal Abuse

In addition to saying things that are meant to be cruel and hurtful, this can be seen when the abuser degrades the victim by cursing or minimizing accomplishments. The abuser may tell the victim that he/she is stupid and unable to function without him/her.

Rigid Sex Roles

The abuser may expect the victim to serve him/her, perhaps saying that the victim must be obedient in all things, including things that are criminal in nature.

Dr. Jekyll & Mr. Hyde

Many victims are confused by their abuser's sudden mood changes. "Explosiveness" and "moodiness" are typical of people who abuse their partners.

Past Abuse

An abuser may admit to battery in the past, but that it was only one time and certainly not his/her fault. The victim may hear from relatives or ex–partners that the person is abusive. Stressful circumstances do not make a person abusive.

Threats of Violence

This includes any threat of physical force meant to control the victim, such as, "I'll knock your head off," "I'm going to kill you," "I'll break your neck." An abuser will try to excuse threats by saying, "Everybody does that."

Breaking or Striking Objects

This behavior is used as punishment (e.g. breaking loved possessions), but is used mostly to terrorize the victim into submission, not only is this a sign of extreme emotional immaturity, but here is great danger when people think they have the right to punish or frighten their partners.

Any Use of Force During an Argument

This may involve an abuser holding a victim down, physically restraining the victim from leaving the room, or any pushing or shoving.

The toll–free domestic abuse hotline is 1–800–799–7233 or 1–800–787–3224 (TTY)

How will you know if an abusive spouse has genuinely changed? To assess whether someone has truly dealt with their abusive behaviour, you first need to determine if they have acknowledged having a problem with anger/violence. If they have, then see if they are willing to discuss their behaviour or if they continue to minimize or deny their abusive behaviour. Are they remorseful or do they feel that their behaviour was some-how justified? Do they show any insight into understanding their behaviour and have they successful completed anger management or counseling or participated in a group for abusers?

Unfortunately, not everyone is motivated to improve their marital relationship. A husband/wife may feel that he/she does not need to change, for example, or they may not be willing to go for marriage counseling. In that case, there are some difficult choices to be considered. A wife/husband can make a decision to stay in the marriage and accept their spouse "as is," knowing he/she may never change (unless they are seriously abusive and then this does not apply). They can suggest a "trial separation" unless their spouse is willing to go to marriage counseling with them, and if necessary, she can go ahead with a "redemptive" separation with the goal of reconciliation.

Ideally, the couple, even though separated, will work on their individual issues and also see someone for marital counseling. Once it has been determined that the major issues are resolved and that the couple have developed effective communication and resolution patterns in their relationship, then they can consider whether a reconciliation would be appropriate.

If you or someone you know is experiencing marriage difficulties, check out www.retrouvaille.org. They have faith–based marriage seminars all over the world that are simply wonderful. These weekends are run by couples who have overcome their own marriage problems and there are follow–up sessions after the weekend to maintain improvements. I have heard the most amazing testimonies of couples who have gone to these weekend seminars, even on the brink of divorce, and their relationship was totally turned around!

I recognize, of course, that even though there is hope for most marriages, that some relationships, for whatever reasons, may end in divorce. It is true that divorce is not the unpardonable sin, even though God wants the best for us and the ideal is to restore relationships if at all possible. I think He must weep when people divorce because of feeble excuses like they as a couple have "drifted apart." If you are divorced and have asked God to forgive you for whatever contribution you have made to the break–up of the marriage, then you are forgiven.

It is still important to learn from our mistakes and to forgive those who have hurt us. Don't ever assume that if you divorce your spouse, that you will eventually find a better mate. Don't rush into any new relationships. It may take a few years after a divorce to thoroughly work through your loss issues, forgiveness, and so forth. Ask God if you can serve Him better as a single person or a married person and tell Him that you will be content with His wisdom in the matter. Then, go forward seeking how to serve Him and fulfill His plan for your life.

It is important for pastors and church members to welcome divorced people. The church can and should play the vital role of restoration and healing of the divorced person. Accepting a divorced person does not mean you condone divorce. Divorced people need to be accepted and loved and Jesus is our example of how to treat these dear ones—remember the woman at the well or the woman caught in adultery? Jesus did not condemn her and challenged those without sin to cast the first stone.

Resources:

Website for abused Christian women—http://www.abuseofwomen.org/

Test your listening skills at www.wittcom.com

Relationship Advice Articles—http://www.neilclarkwarren.com/articles.html & http://www.neilclarkwarren.com/advice.html

Covenant Marriage, the Five Love Languages–
by Gary Chapman

Growing through Divorce—Jim Smoke (study guide used for separated/divorce groups)

Retrouvaille (rediscovery)—Christian Experience to Alleviate Marriage Breakdown—communication seminars—www.retrouvaille.org

The Christ–Centered Marriage—Neil T. Anderson

A Lasting Promise: The Christian Guide to Fighting for Your Marriage—Scott Stanley, Daniel Trathen, Savanna McCain, B. Milton Bryan

Marriage Conflicts—Everett Worthington and Douglas McMurry

SELF–ESTEEM

If you don't truly believe that you are as valuable and as loveable as anyone else, then you may be suffering from low self–esteem and/or a poor self–image. Do you still like yourself even when others reject you? Do you love and support yourself no matter what happens or regardless of what others say about you? Some Christians that are talented and totally capable of having successful careers and healthy relationships will actually sabotage anything positive in their lives because, way deep down inside, they don't really believe that they deserve good things happening to them.

Enriching Self–esteem

Self–esteem is essential for personal growth. I came across the verse "love your neighbour as you love yourself" ten times in the Bible. To truly love others, you need to love yourself. Not in a conceited, proud way, of course, but in a healthy, positive way. We are not to think that we are better than anyone else but it is just as important that we don't think we are of any less value than anyone else. We are children of God most high and we need to really appreciate what that means. We need to be confident because of who we are in Christ. No one will ever love you so completely and as unconditionally as God loves you. If you are able to accept His love, then you will come to understand that you can love yourself and then you can love others to the best of your ability as well.

Unfortunately, many Christians suffer from low self-esteem. It's important to know that not everyone in your entire life will like you, no matter what you look like or how you act or how much money you have, etc. There will always be someone who just doesn't approve of you, for whatever reason, and it is usually more about their own issues anyway. The sooner we accept this fact, the sooner we can let go of trying to gain everyone's approval.

If you are being yourself, and someone still doesn't like you, then it is their loss and you don't need people like that as your friend anyway. The truth is that you don't need everyone to like you and you don't need anyone's approval. Decide to love and accept yourself as is, even if no one else ever does. Be your own best friend, in other words. Be your biggest cheerleader. Be your own loving parent if you didn't have that as a child. Be kind to yourself. Be good to yourself. Take care of yourself. Make healthy choices for yourself. Nurture yourself. Be patient with yourself. Treat yourself the way you would want others to treat you. I like what Eleanor Roosevelt said, "No one can make you feel inferior without your permission." This is so true. We tell others how they can treat us by the way we respond to them.

When people say hurtful things to you, you can imagine an arrow aimed at your heart, only visualize an invisible shield that repels the arrow and sends it back. You don't have to accept the criticism so don't take it to heart. On the other hand, if you examine yourself and find it to be true about yourself, resolve to make improvements and forgive yourself for being human.

We need to strengthen our identity as beloved children of God. Read these verses over slowly, prayerfully, with conviction, and out loud to get a sense of what it really means to belong to Jesus, to be victorious in Him, to be a joint heir with Him.

Who I am In Christ

By Neil T. Anderson[61]

- I am a child of God (John 1:12)

- I have peace with God (Romans 5:1)

- The Holy Spirit lives in me (1 Corinthians 3:16)

- I have access to God's wisdom (James 1:5)

- I am helped by God (Hebrews 4:16)

- I am reconciled to God (Romans 5:11)

- I am not condemned by God (Romans 8:1)

- I am justified (Romans 5:1)

- I have Christ's righteousness
  (Romans 5:19; 2 Corinthians 5:21)

- I am Christ's ambassador (2 Corinthians 5:20)

- I am completely forgiven (Colossians 1:14)

- I am tenderly loved by God (Jeremiah 31:3)

- I am the sweet fragrance of Christ to God
  (2 Corinthians 2:15)

- I am a temple in which God dwells (1 Corinthians 3:16)

- I am blameless and beyond reproach (Colossians 1:22)

- I am the salt of the earth (Matthew 5:13)

- I am the light of the world (Matthew 5:14)
- I am a branch on Christ's vine (John 15:15)
- I am Christ's friend (John 15:5)
- I am chosen by Christ to bear fruit (John 15:6)
- I am a joint heir with Christ, sharing his inheritance with him (Romans 8:17)
- I am united to the Lord, one spirit with Him (1 Corinthians 6:17)
- I am a member of Christ's body (1 Corinthians 12:27)
- I am a saint (Ephesians 1:1)
- I am hidden with Christ in God (Colossians 3:3)
- I am chosen by God, holy and dearly loved (Colossians 3:12)
- I am a child of the light (1 Thessalonians 5:5)
- I am holy, and I share in God's heavenly calling (Hebrews 3:1)
- I am sanctified (Hebrews 2:11)
- I am one of God's living stones, being built up in Christ as a spiritual house (1 Peter 2:5)
- I am a member of a chosen race, a royal priesthood, a holy nation, a people for God's own possession and created to sing his praises (1 Peter 2:9– 10)
- I am firmly rooted and built up in Christ (Colossians 2:7)
- I am born of God, and the evil one cannot touch me (1 John 5:18)

- I have the mind of Christ (1 Corinthians 2:16)
- I may approach God with boldness, freedom, and confidence (Ephesians 3:12)
- I have been rescued from Satan's domain and transferred into the kingdom of Christ (Colossians 1:13)
- I have been made complete in Christ (Colossians 2:10)
- I have been given a spirit of power, love, and self–discipline (2 Timothy 1:7)
- I have been given great and precious promises by God (2 Peter 1:4)
- My needs are met by God (Philippians 4:19)
- I am a prince (princess) in God's kingdom (John 1:12; 1 Timothy 6:15)
- I have been bought with a price, and I belong to God (1 Corinthians 6:19,20)
- I have been adopted as God's child (Ephesians 1:5)
- I have direct access to God through the Holy Spirit (Ephesians 2:18)
- I am assured that all things are working together for good (Romans 8:28)
- I am free from any condemning charges against me (Romans 8:31)
- I cannot be separated from the love of God (Romans 8:35)

- I have been established, anointed, and sealed by God (2 Corinthians 1:21,22)

- I am confident that the good work that God has begun in me will be perfected (Philippians 1:6)

- I am a citizen of heaven (Philippians 3:20)

- I am a personal witness of Christ's (Acts 1:8)

- I am God's co–worker (2 Corinthians 6:1, 1 Corinthians 3:9)

- I am seated with Christ in the heavenly realm (Ephesians 2:6)

- I am God's workmanship (Ephesians 2:10)

- I can do all things through Christ, who gives me the strength I need (Philippians 4:13)

In order to change years of negative thinking about yourself, you need to renew your mind (Romans 12: 2). This means replacing negative, defeating, self–depreciative thoughts with uplifting, nurturing, thoughts *every* time you start to get down on yourself and then support the new way of thinking with verses from the Word of God—the truth. This is known as biblical cognitive therapy.

Steps to Change Negative Thinking Patterns

1. Train yourself to become aware of what you are thinking anytime you feel a negative emotion.

2. As soon as you become aware of any negative thoughts, stop those thoughts immediately.

3. Replace the negative thoughts with positive, nurturing thoughts. If you can't think of anything right away, try to think of what you would say to encourage your best friend in the same situation.

4. Look up or quote a Bible verse that supports the positive statements to reinforce the truth about yourself (affirmations). Personalize the verse so that you apply it to yourself, so instead of, "For you are my offspring" (Acts 17:28), say, "I am God's offspring."

Example One

"I failed that test. I am dumb. I can never do anything right," is replaced with, "I am human. It is okay to make mistakes. I will do better next time. Even though I failed the test, I am of infinite worth in God's sight." And then quote a verse such as, "I have access to God's wisdom" (James 1:5).

Example Two

"I am so nervous about doing this presentation. I just know I am going to mess it up. I am not good at public speaking and everyone will see that. I will look like a fool," is replaced with, "I have practiced this presentation and I am going to do it to the best of my ability and leave the outcome to God." And then quote a verse like, "I can do all things through Christ, who gives me the strength I need" (Philippians 4:13).

Example Three

"I am anxious about meeting my new co–workers. I want everyone to like me." is replaced with, "I will be myself and everyone may not approve of me, and if they don't it's okay because God loves me and I accept myself. It's impossible to gain everybody's approval anyway and I would only want people who truly appreciate me to be my friend in any case." And then quote a verse such as, "I am tenderly loved by God" (Jeremiah 31:3) or, "I am God's treasured possession" (Exodus 19:5).

Example Four

"I am fat and no one would want me for their girlfriend," is replaced with, "Even though I am overweight, God loves me just as I am and I accept myself just as I am. If God wants me to be in a relationship, then the right person will appreciate me as I am. My worth is not dependent on another's approval." And then quote a verse like, "I am fearfully and wonderfully made" (Psalm 139) or, "And it is my desire to lavish my love on you" (1 John 3:1).

Of course these exercises are only effective if you practice them consistently. You may have negative "tapes" from your childhood to correct as well such as, "I can't feel worthwhile unless a certain condition is met." It is a lie that we can only be happy "if I am married" or "if I am attractive" or "if I am successful," etc.

Many people, especially those who have been abused as children, believe the core belief that they are inadequate or that they don't deserve success, love, or happiness. Notice how many of these lies affect your self–esteem. Notice how many make an external condition a requirement for worth or happiness. Tell yourself the opposite of these lies every day for one week and then check your core beliefs again.

The key is to counteract each of these negative beliefs with the truth about yourself—you are of infinite value to God and there is nothing you can do or not do to make God love you any more or any less than He does at this very moment. He will always love you, so you can rest in the knowledge of His love. Romans 8:39, "For I am persuaded, that neither death, nor life, nor angels, nor principalities, nor powers, nor things present, nor things to come, nor height, nor depth, nor any other creature, shall be able to separate us from the love of God, which is in Christ Jesus our Lord."

Make a list of your strengths and create opportunities for yourself to demonstrate those strengths. Take risks—the more you do something, the more confident you become about your skills.

Resources:

www.fathersloveletter.com

Ten Days to Self–Esteem by David Burns

Building Self–Esteem: A 125 Day Program,
by Glenn R. Schiraldi, Ph.D.,

Self–esteem Comes in All Sizes: How to be Happy at your Natural Weight by Carol A. Johnson

Eating Disorders

When we let eating or not eating dominate our life and we are more concerned about our physical shape than we are about our spiritual and emotional health, our thinking is out of balance and we are placing priority on our relationship with food or making an idol of our body. Deuteronomy 5:7–8 declares, "Have no other gods before me. You shall not make for yourself an idol in the form of anything."

Anorexia (starving oneself) and bulimia (binging and purging) are the most well known forms of eating disorders. People who suffer from eating disorders often have a distorted body image, low self–esteem, and a need to be perfect. Eating disorders are largely about control issues. Often people with eating disorders succumb to media and peer pressure regarding body ideals. They may come from dysfunctional families with patterns of enmeshment, overprotection, conflict avoidance, and impossible expectations. Do any of these apply to you and how?

Pleasers try to belong by keeping the peace but then they can't express their true feelings. Controllers think they can achieve a sense of acceptance by maintaining maximum control of themselves and possibly others. They may achieve this perceived sense of control through the attention focused on their illness.

Christians with eating disorders are not looking to God for their sense of worth and identity; they erringly seek significance and belonging with thinness and performance. Unfortunately, they do not accept God's unconditional love for them and so they struggle with feelings of rejection, guilt, and helplessness. They may be pre–occupied with a need to please and control. Medical treatment is necessary to promote physical and emotional health. Spiritual restoration is also needed to achieve a positive self–image and to strengthen their identity in Christ.

The Bible says in 1 Corinthians 3:16–17, "Don't you know that you yourselves are God's temple and that God's Spirit lives in you? If anyone destroys God's temple, God will destroy him: for God's temple is sacred, and you are that temple." Pretty strong warning there, but it's because God loves us and wants the best for us. You deserve to be healthy in your body, mind, and soul. It will not help you to stuff or restrict feelings with food to avoid the expression of negative emotions.

Recovery begins when you acknowledge your worth in Christ and when you can accept God's love for you and learn to love yourself, you will understand that you do not need to perform in any way to be accepted. Jesus died for us all because we were imperfect, and because He died for us, we do not need to be perfect: "It is finished" (John 19:30). God wants you to be a healthy member of the body of Christ and He wants you to take care of your physical body, the temple of the Holy Spirit that He gave you. Searching for worth in thinness, performance, and/or control will never provide the wholeness that is only found when you claim your identity in Christ.

If you have an eating disorder, it is unlikely that you will be able to overcome it on your own. Make sure you seek the support of a professional who has expertise in eating disorders. You will need to develop more effective coping strategies, increase your self–esteem, identify and work through your feelings, strengthen your identity in Christ, correct your body image, and replace negative thinking. It would be beneficial if you could also participate in family therapy to explore how family members may be maintaining the dysfunctional/emotional patterns and to define their role in your recovery.

My thirty–eight–year–old cousin died as a result of destroying her liver through an eating disorder. You need to be under the care of a physician to ensure that you are not experiencing any nutritional deficiencies or other effects of eating disorders

Prayer for Those who have Eating Disorders and/or have Cut Themselves

by Neil T. Anderson [62]

"I renounce the lie that my value as a person is dependent on my physical beauty, my weight, or my size. I renounce cutting myself, vomiting, using laxatives, or starving myself as a means of trying to cleanse myself of evil or alter my appearance. I announce that only the blood of Jesus Christ cleanses me from sin. I accept the reality that there may be sin present in me due to the lies I have believed and the wrongful use of my body is evil, but I renounce the lie that I am evil or that any part of my body is evil. My body is the temple of the Holy Spirit and I belong to you, Lord Jesus. I receive your love and acceptance of me. Heal me now, in Jesus' name. Amen"

Resources:

Chapters in this book: Accepting God's Love, Self–esteem.

A free online course for eating disorders can be found at www.settingcaptivesfree.com– click on "food issues" and then "In His Image"

These are eating disorder hotlines and the first one is open 24 hours: 1–800–382–2832

1–800–762–3334

1–800–227–4785

www.remudaranch.com Arizona christian eating disorder treatment centre

1–800–445–1900

www.something–fishy.org Monthly chat groups sessions and chat sessions

www.edauk.com Helpline, how to help a friend, etc

Seeing Yourself in God's Image: Overcoming anorexia and Bullemia by Martha Homme

Steps to Freedom in Christ by Neil T. Anderson

Twenty Ways to Love Your Body –http://www.nationaleat-ingdisorders.org/p.asp?WebPage_ID=320&Profile_ID=41160

SELF–INJURY

It may surprise some to know that there are Christians out there that hurt themselves physically. Self–injury is distinguished from suicide attempts in that suicide is an attempt to end one's life and self–injury is a method of coping with intense emotional pain. Self–injury can involve many activities; however, cutting, burning, and hitting are the most common.

Favazza and Conterio [63]two leading researchers on self–injury, believe that self–injury affects 2 to 8 million Americans per year so it's not as rare as one would think. Many of those who self–injure choose to harm parts of their bodies that they would normally cover up with everyday clothing. Most experts agree that there may be some that self–harm for attention; however, Jan Sutton sums it up well when she says in her book *Healing the Hurt Within*[64] that, "Self–harm is rarely attention–seeking. Perhaps a more apt description might be 'attention needing.'"

Why do people self–injure? For many, many different reasons. In her book *Women Living With Self–Injury*, Jane Hyman [65]lists twenty–five different reasons for self–injuring! Some of the most common are to release emotions, to show hatred for oneself, to calm racing thoughts or stop flashbacks. Hospitalization is necessary in extreme cases to stabilize someone so that they are able to benefit from therapy.

Studies by Hughes and Kosterlitz[66] have shown that when you are injured, regardless of how you sustained the injury, the body reacts by immediately releasing endorphins to help the body cope with the injury. It is a chemical reaction that may cause a person to feel comforted and soothed. In fact, morphine, relieves pain because it mimics the behavior of your body's own endorphins. So self–injury is often a way of self–medicating to relieve pain and comfort oneself.

To overcome self–injury, you need to learn to look to God to meet your emotional needs for comfort. You may have to seek professional counseling to deal with unresolved issues from the past, and you need to develop new ways of expressing yourself and what you are feeling in ways that are not harmful to yourself.

Try to identify what feelings make you want to self–injure, your personal triggers: disappointment, rejection, poor self–image, and so forth and ask God to comfort you. Read my chapters on self–esteem and accepting God's love. Use positive affirmations and Bible verses to talk yourself out of cutting.

In Leviticus 19:28, we are warned, "Do not cut your bodies for the dead or put tattoo marks on yourselves. I am the Lord." This is because our bodies are the temple of the Holy Spirit (1 Corinthians 6:19, 20). You dishonor God with your body if you self–injure, as it is an act of defacing God's image within you. Even so, God loves you with a tender love and will help you to deal with your pain in other ways.

www.self–injury.org is a Christian Web site that provides a whole list of activities to do instead of cutting. They also have a great article on ending self–injury. Expect setbacks, but get right back on track. See a Christian therapist to help you explore the issues that led to self–injury who can support you in overcoming it. Pray the prayer at the end of Eating Disorders. You may also be able to find a self–injury support group in your area.

Resources:

www.selfinjury.com SAFE—Self–abuse finally ends. 1–800–dont–cut (366–8288)

http://www.sisupport.org/

http://www.bpdresources.com/selfinjury.html

http://groups.msn.com/SelfHarmSelfInjurySupportRoom— Online support chat room.

http://christians–in–recovery.org—lists books on overcoming self–injury

SINGLES

I can personally identify with singles who contact me for help in dealing with being a single Christian. For years, it was a problem for me to accept not being married. I now warn people about not letting finding a partner become an "idol" in their lives. The best way to pray about this issue is to tell God that you are willing to serve Him in the way that He sees best for your life, whether that is being married or not. If He can use you best for His glory and purposes as a single person, then so be it.

It is normal to want to have a life partner; however, if you start resenting God when you find that you continue to be single, it can create a problem in your relationship with God. It is so hard sometimes to trust in God's love for us, to believe that He knows what is best for us, but He really does and we have to choose to believe that.

It is important to have a good support system as a single person whether it be family member(s), friends from work, friends at church, in your community, etc. A lot of the need for belonging and acceptance can come from other people besides a wife or husband. Ask yourself what your academic, professional, and personal goals would be if you knew that you would never marry or remarry, and then set out to achieve those goals.

If you believe that God has someone in the future for you, then set out to be the best marriage partner you can be and work on areas of self–improvement that you can think of in preparation for meeting the right person.

If you haven't read *The Purpose Driven Life* by Rick Warren, get a copy and discover what your true focus should be: on spreading the gospel and ministering to others. The need for giving love and receiving love can be fulfilled through ministry to others. If you are involved in a ministry that involves an emotional investment from you, you often find that you are the one that ends up being ministered to as well. In giving love and help to others, you fulfill a need of your own.

Pets can help a great deal. Studies have shown that petting an animal actually changes the serotonin levels in your brain. Pets love you unconditionally. They look forward to your return home and you mean everything to them. They also meet a need you may have to nurture someone else.

Take advantage of your single years by doing all those things like missions that involve travel that you might not be able to do as easily with a partner and children.

There may be many reasons why God may not give you a partner. It does not mean that He loves you any less than anyone else. He may want you to have a deeper, closer relationship with Him. He may feel that you need to be more established in your faith first, or there might be some personal growth or healing He wants you to experience before you make that commitment. It may be that the right person for you doesn't know the Lord yet or it is just not the right time to meet them. For every minute you remain single, trust that it is in your best interest based on a good and loving reason by a good and loving God.

We are told in 1 Corinthians 7:1–2, "A man does well not to marry but because there is so much immorality, every man should have his own wife, and every woman should have her own husband," and then later in verse 8–9, "Now, to the unmarried and to the widows I say that it would be better for you to continue to live alone as I do. But if you cannot restrain your desires, go ahead and marry– it is better to marry than to burn with passion."

In the same chapter in verse 32–34 Paul states, "I would like you to be free from every worry. An unmarried man concerns himself with the Lord's work because he is trying to please the Lord. But a married man concerns himself with worldly matters because he wants to please his wife, and so he is pulled in two directions." It is summed up best in verse 38, "The man who marries does well, but the one who doesn't does even better."

So married people should thank God for such a blessing and rejoice in their relationship with their spouse. If you are single, however, rejoice in your relationship with the Lord and be thankful that you are more available to Him and for Him. Perhaps because singles rely on Him alone; they may also have the opportunity to develop more emotional and spiritual intimacy with Him. That's not to say married people don't have deep, personal relationships with the Lord, of course, but there truly are benefits to being single and a higher purpose for us, at least for the time being.

If you are single, know that your worth and attractiveness has nothing to do with whether or not you are in a relationship.

You are already a princess even though God may still be preparing your prince and you are already a prince even though God may be still preparing your princess. "Ye are complete in Him, which is the head of all principality and power" (Colossians 2:10).

Scriptural Encouragement:

For I am your provider and I meet all your needs.

Matthew 6:31–33

My plan for your future has always been filled with hope.

Jeremiah 29:11

Because I love you with an everlasting love.

Jeremiah 31:3

My thoughts toward you are countless as the sand on the seashore.

Psalm 139:17–18

And I rejoice over you with singing.

Zephaniah 3:17

I will never stop doing good to you.

Jeremiah 32:40

For you are my treasured possession.

Exodus 19:5

I desire to establish you with all my heart and all my soul.

Jeremiah 32:41

If you seek me with all your heart, you will find me.

Deuteronomy 4:29

Prayer for Singles by Liberty Savard[67]

Father, I bind myself to your will and purposes for my future. I want your plans to be fulfilled in my life, whether they are the plans I think I want or not. You know the tug on my heart when I see a loving husband and wife. I long for such a relationship, but if I desire a mate only to fill an empty place in my heart instead of seeking to fill it with You, show me how to change. I bind myself to pure motives for wanting a mate, not just to meet my unmet needs, to heal my unhealed hurts, and to help me resolve all my unresolved issues. That is placing unrealistic expectations on any human. No man or woman could ever fulfil such expectations. You alone can do that. You alone can fill me with grace, bathe me in love, meet my needs, heal my hurts, and resolve my questions and issues.

I loose the layers of self–projection and self–defense I have laid down over these areas of vulnerability in my life. Jesus, I want to let you get to these sources of my neediness and loneliness and pain so you can heal them with your supernatural power, grace, mercy, and love. Only you can fix this all–consuming feeling that I'm trapped in a vacuum where nothing comes to me is ever enough. I don't want to be needy and hurting. I want to be a source of hope and blessing to others. No one will get hope from watching a life that is always unfulfilled, needy, and in pain. But I know that many can receive hope from a life that was once like that, but has now been changed and made whole by You.

I long for You to do whatever You need to do to heal me, meet my needs, and fix me with your love. I loose the control from my soul that kept You from doing this. I do not want to force my way past your will into a relationship only to see my needs suck all the joy, peace, and life out of a mate. Lord, forgive me for the times I have blamed You for my loneliness, my lack of having someone to care for me.

I know that you have been protecting me and others from the hurt and heartbreak a wrong relationship brings. I loose all of the discouragement, deception, and denial from my soul that has kept You from getting into its deepest parts—the places so dark and lonely that I won't even go there. Lord, I will let you fix me in whatever way You need to fix me.

Jesus, if there is a special man/woman you have chosen and are preparing just for me, I bind him/her to your will and purposes. I ask that you draw him/her into a strong, whole relationship with You, Jesus. I ask that you teach him/her to see you as the focus and very centre of his/her life, just as I am asking You to do with me. I bind myself and him/her to your timing. You will know when the time is right for both of us to come together in the relationship You choose.

Lord, if you desire for me to remain wholly devoted to and single–minded toward you, then pour your grace and mercy into me and mark me as yours alone. Teach me how to come into a covenant of intimacy with You like I have never been before.

Teach me to hear your voice and respond to every word of your love. Teach me how to love You, to bless You, to minister to You. Teach me how to come apart from the world and go with You into that never–yet–entered secret meeting place that is just ours. Teach me how to receive whatever You want to give to me. I bind and loose these things in Jesus' name."

I thank you for the keys of the Kingdom in Matthew 16:19, which You have given me authority to bind and loose on earth, according to Your will, and they will be bound and loosed in heaven. Thank you, Lord, for the truth and promise of your Word. In Jesus' name."

MEANING IN SUFFERING—
CHAPTER BY KURT DE HAAN[68]

It's an old question. Four thousand years ago, a victim of personal, family, and financial reversals spoke to the silent heavens and pleaded, "Show me why You contend with me. Does it seem good to You that You should oppress, that You should despise the work of Your hands?" (Job 10: 2,3,8). The questions are still being asked. "Does God hate me? Is this why He is allowing me to suffer like this? Why me and not others?"

There are answers. Not exhaustive, but enough to keep our pain in perspective. Enough to show us how to put suffering to work for us. In the following pages, RBC staff writer Kurt De Haan shows us that while heaven may not be answering all our questions, it is giving us all the answers we need to trust and love the One who, in our pain, is calling us to Himself.

Elusive Answers

Life can be hard to understand. In trying to come to grips with the cold realities of our existence, we can easily become frustrated. We long for answers to the immense problem of suffering. We may even wonder if we will ever fully comprehend why bad things happen to good people and why good things happen to bad people. The answers often seem to be elusive, hidden, out of reach.

Oh, it makes sense that a terrorist would be killed by his own bomb. It makes sense that a reckless driver would be in a serious accident. It makes sense that a person who plays with fire would get burned. It even makes sense that a chain smoker would develop lung cancer. But what about the innocent men, women, and children who are killed by a terrorist's bomb? What about the young driver who suffers severe brain damage because a drunk veered over the center line? What about the person whose home burns down due to no fault of his own? And what about the two–year–old child with leukemia?

It is dangerous, even foolish, to pretend that we have a complete answer as to why God allows suffering. The reasons are many and complex. It's just as wrong to demand that we should understand. When the Old Testament sufferer Job realized that he had no right to demand an answer from God, he said, "Therefore I have uttered what I did not understand, things too wonderful for me, which I did not know" (Job 42:3).

But God has given us some answers. Although we may not be able to know why one person gets singled out for a disease, we can know part of the reason why diseases exist. And even though we may not understand why we face a certain problem, we can know how to deal with the situation and respond in a way that pleases the Lord.

One more thing. I am not going to pretend that I fully understand the suffering that you personally may be experiencing. Although some aspects of human pain are common, the particulars are different. And what you may need most right now is not a four–point outline on why you are suffering or even what to do about it. What you may need most is a hug, a listening ear, or someone who will just sit with you in silence.

Sometime along the way, however, you will want and need the truths of God's Word to comfort you and help you to see your plight from God's perspective. You and I need more than untested theories. That's why in the pages that follow I have tried to include the insights of people who have suffered a variety of physical and emotional pains. My prayer for you is that your faith in God will stand firm even when your world seems to be falling apart.

Why Would A Good God Allow Suffering?

In our world of pain, where is God? If He is good and compassionate, why is life often so tragic? Has He lost control? Or, if He is in control, what is He trying to do to me and to others? Some people have chosen to deny God's existence because they cannot imagine a God who would allow such misery. Some believe that God exists, but they want nothing to do with Him because they don't think He could be good. Others have settled for a belief in a kindly God who loves us but has lost control of a rebellious planet. Still others cling tenaciously to a belief in an all–wise, all–powerful, loving God who somehow uses evil for good.

As we search the Bible, we discover that it paints a picture of a God who can do anything He chooses to do. Sometimes He has acted in mercy and performed miracles in behalf of His people. At other times, though, He has chosen to do nothing to stop tragedy. He is supposed to be intimately involved in our lives, yet at times He seems deaf to our cries for help. In the Bible, He assures us that He controls all that happens, but He sometimes let's us be the targets of evil people, bad genes, dangerous viruses, or natural disasters.

If you're like me, you long for some way to put together an answer to this puzzling issue of suffering. I believe that God has given us enough pieces of the puzzle to help us trust Him even when we don't have all the information we would like. In this brief study we will see that the basic answers of the Bible are that our good God allows pain and suffering in our world to alert us to the problem of sin, to direct us to respond to Him in faith and hope, to shape us to be more like Christ, and to unite us so that we will help each other.

Why Would God Allow Suffering—To Alert Us

Imagine a world without pain. What would it be like? At first the idea may sound appealing. No more headaches. No more backaches. No more upset stomachs. No more throbbing sensations when the hammer misses the mark and lands on your thumb. No more sore throats. But there would also be no more sensation to alert you of a broken bone or tearing ligaments. No alarm to let you know that an ulcer is eating a hole in your stomach. No discomfort to warn of a cancerous tumour that is gathering forces for a takeover of your body. No angina to let you know that the blood vessels to your heart are clogging up. No pain to signal a ruptured appendix.

As much as we may abhor pain, we have to admit that it often serves a good purpose. It warns us when something goes wrong. The cause of the misery, rather than the agony itself, is the real problem. Pain is merely a symptom, a siren or bell that sounds when a part of the body is endangered or under attack. In this section we will see how pain could be God's way to alert us that:

1. Something's wrong with the world.

2. Something's wrong with God's creatures.

3. Something's wrong with me.

Any one of these problems could be the reason for the pain in our lives. Let's look at each possible diagnosis.

1. Something's Wrong with the World

The sorry condition of our planet indicates that something has gone terribly wrong. The suffering we experience and the distress we sense in others indicate that suffering does not discriminate on the basis of race, social status, religion, or even morality. It can seem cruel, random, purposeless, grotesque, and wildly out of control. Bad things happen to people who try to be good, and good things happen to people who enjoy being bad.

The seeming unfairness of it all has struck close to each of us. I remember watching my grandmother as she was dying of cancer. Grandma and Grandpa Blohm moved in with our family. My mother, a registered nurse, took care of her during her final months. Mom administered the pain killer. Grandpa desperately wanted her to be healed. Then the day came when the hearse pulled up and took away her frail, wasted body. I knew she was in heaven, but it still hurt. I hated cancer—I still do.

As I sit here thinking of all the suffering that my friends, co-workers, family, neighbours, and church family have experienced, I can hardly believe the length of the list—and my list is incomplete. So often these people have suffered through no apparent fault of their own. An accident, a birth defect, a genetic disorder, a miscarriage, an abusive parent, chronic pain, a rebellious child, a severe illness, random disease, the death of a spouse or a child, a broken relationship, a natural disaster. It just doesn't seem fair. From time to time I'm tempted to give in to frustration.

How do we resolve this? How do we live with the cold facts of life without denying reality or being overcome with despair? Couldn't God have created a world where nothing would ever go wrong? Couldn't He have made a world where people would never have the ability to make a bad choice or ever hurt another person? Couldn't He have made a world where mosquitoes, weeds, and cancer would never exist? He could have, but He didn't.

The great gift of human freedom that He has given to us, the ability to choose, carries with it the risk of making wrong choices. If you could choose between being a free thinking creature in a world where bad choices produce suffering, or being a robot in a world without pain, what would you decide? What kind of being would bring more honour to God? What kind of creature would love Him more?

We could have been created to be like the cute battery-operated dolls that say "I love you" when hugged. But God had other plans. He took a "risk" to create beings who could do the unthinkable: rebel against their Creator. What happened in paradise? Temptation, bad choices, and tragic consequences destroyed the tranquillity of Adam and Eve's existence. Genesis 2 and 3 detail how Satan tested their love for the Lord—and they failed. In biblical terms, that failure is called sin. And just as the AIDS virus infects a body, breaks down the body's immune system, and leads to death, so also sin spreads as a deadly infection that passes from one generation to the next. Each new generation inherits the effects of sin and the desire to sin (Romans 1:18–32; 5:12,15,18).

Not only did the entrance of sin into the world have devastating effects on the nature of human beings, but sin also brought about immediate and continual judgment from God. Genesis 3 relates how physical and spiritual death became a part of human existence (vv.3,19), childbirth became painful (v.16), the ground was cursed with weeds that would make man's work very difficult (vv.17–19), and Adam and Eve were evicted from the special Garden where they had enjoyed intimate fellowship with God (vv.23,24).

In the New Testament, the apostle Paul described the whole creation of God as groaning and eagerly anticipating the time when it will be freed from the curse of decay and be remade, free from the effects of sin (Romans 8:19–22). Disease, disaster, and corruption are symptoms of a deeper problem: the human race has rebelled against the Creator. Every sorrow, grief, and agony is a vivid reminder of our human predicament. Like a huge neon sign, the reality of suffering screams the message that the world is not the way God created it to be.

Therefore, the first and most basic answer to the problem of the existence of suffering is that it is the direct result of sin's entrance into the world. Pain alerts us that a spiritual disease is wracking our planet. Many times our troubles may be merely the side–effects of living in a fallen world, through no direct fault of our own.

2. Something's Wrong with God's Creatures

We can be targets of cruel acts from other people or from Satan's rebel army. Both fallen human beings and fallen spirit beings (angels who have rebelled) have the capacity to make decisions that damage themselves and others. Suffering can be caused by people. As free (and sin–infected) creatures, people have made and will continue to make many bad choices in life. These bad choices often affect other people.

For example, one of Adam's sons, Cain, made a choice to kill his brother Abel (Genesis 4:7,8). Lamech boasted about his violence (vv.23,24). Sarai mistreated Hagar (Genesis 16:1–6). Laban swindled his nephew Jacob (Genesis 29:15–30). Joseph's brothers sold him into slavery (Genesis 37:12–36), and then Potiphar's wife falsely accused him of attempted rape and had him thrown into prison (Genesis 39). Pharaoh cruelly mistreated the Jewish slaves in Egypt (Exodus 1). King Herod slaughtered all the babies who lived in and around Bethlehem in an attempt to kill Jesus (Matthew 2:16–18).

The hurt that others inflict on us may be due to selfishness on their part. Or you may be the target of persecution because of your faith in Christ. Throughout history, people who have identified with the Lord have suffered at the hands of those who rebelled against God. Before his conversion, Saul was a rabid anti–Christian who did all he could to make life miserable for believers—even working to have them put to death (Acts 7:54–8:3). But after his dramatic turn to the Lord Jesus, he bravely endured all types of persecution as he boldly proclaimed the gospel message (2 Corinthians 4:7–12; 6:1–10). He could even say that the suffering he endured helped to make him more like Christ (Philippians 3:10).

Suffering can also be caused by Satan and demons. Job's life story is a vivid example of how a good person can suffer incredible tragedy because of a satanic attack. God allowed Satan to take away Job's possessions, his family, and his health (Job 1,2). I cringed even as I wrote the preceding sentence. Somehow, and for His reasons, God allowed Satan to devastate Job's life. We may tend to compare what God did to Job to a father who allows the neighbourhood bully to beat up his children just to see if they would still love Dad afterward. But, as Job came to realize, that's not a fair assessment when speaking about our wise and loving God.

We know, though Job did not, that his life was a test case, a living testimonial to the trustworthiness of God. Job illustrated that a person can trust God and maintain integrity even when life falls apart (for whatever reason) because God is worth trusting. In the end, Job learned that even though he didn't understand what God was up to, he had plenty of reason to believe that God was not being unjust, cruel, sadistic, or unfair by allowing his life to be ripped apart (Job 42).

The apostle Paul experienced a physical problem that he attributed to Satan. He called it a "thorn in the flesh…, a messenger of Satan to buffet me" (2 Corinthians 12:7). Paul prayed to be freed from the problem, but God didn't give him what he asked for. Instead, the Lord helped him to see how this difficulty could serve a good purpose. It made Paul humbly dependent on the Lord and put him in a position to experience His grace (vv.8–10). Although most cases of sickness cannot be directly tied to Satan's work, the gospel accounts do record a few examples of suffering attributed to Satan, including a blind and mute man (Matthew12:22) and a boy who suffered seizures (17:14–18).

3. Something's Wrong with Me

Too often when something goes wrong in our lives we immediately jump to the conclusion that God is whipping us because of some sin we've committed. That's not necessarily true. As we indicated in the previous points, much of the suffering that comes into our lives is because we live in a broken world inhabited by broken people and rebellious spirit beings.

Job's friends mistakenly thought that he was suffering because of sin in his life (Job 4:7,8; 8:1–6; 22:4,5; 36:17). Jesus' own disciples jumped to the wrong conclusion when they saw a blind man. They wondered if the man's eye problem was due to his personal sin or because of something his parents had done (John 9:1,2). Jesus told them that the man's physical problem was not related to his personal sin or the sin of his parents (v.3).

With these cautions in mind, we need to deal with the hard truth that some suffering does come as the direct consequence of sin, either as corrective discipline from God for those He loves, or punitive action by God upon rebels in His universe. Correction. If you and I have placed our trust in Jesus Christ as our Saviour, then we are children of God. As such, we are part of a family headed by a loving Father who trains and corrects us. He's not an abusive, sadistic parent who dishes out severe beatings because He gets some twisted pleasure out of it. Hebrews 12 states: "My son, do not despise the chastening of the Lord, nor be discouraged when you are rebuked by Him; for whom the Lord loves He chastens, and scourges every son whom He receives. Furthermore, we have had human fathers who corrected us, and we paid them respect. Shall we not much more readily be in subjection to the Father of spirits and live? For they indeed for a few days chastened us as seemed best to them, but He for our profit, that we may be partakers of His holiness" (Hebrews 12:5,6,9,10). And to the church in Laodicea, Jesus said, "As many as I love, I rebuke and chasten. Therefore be zealous and repent" (Revelation 3:19).

King David knew what it was like to experience the tough love of the Lord. After his adultery with Bathsheba and his conniving to ensure that her husband would be killed in battle, David did not repent until the prophet Nathan confronted him. Psalm 51 recounts David's struggle with guilt and his cry for forgiveness. In another psalm, David reflected on the effects of covering up and ignoring sin. He wrote, "When I kept silent, my bones grew old through my groaning all the day long. For day and night Your hand was heavy upon me" (Psalm 32:3,4).

In 1 Corinthians 11:27–32, the apostle Paul warned believers that treating the things of the Lord lightly—partaking of the Lord's Supper without taking it seriously—will bring discipline. Paul explained that this discipline of the Lord was purposeful. He said, "But when we are judged, we are chastened by the Lord, that we may not be condemned with the world" (v.32).

Most of us can understand the principle that whom God loves He disciplines. We would expect a loving Father to correct us and call us to renew our obedience to Him. Judgment. God also acts to deal with stubborn unbelievers who persist in doing evil. A person who has not received God's gift of salvation can expect to receive God's wrath at a future day of judgment and the danger of harsh judgment now if He so chooses.

The Lord brought the flood to destroy decadent humanity (Genesis 6). He destroyed Sodom and Gomorrah (Genesis 18,19). He sent plagues on the Egyptians (Exodus 7–12). He commanded Israel to completely destroy the pagans who inhabited the Promised Land (Deuteronomy 7:1–3). He struck down the arrogant King Herod of New Testament times (Acts 12:19–23). And at the future day of judgment, God will deal out perfect justice to all those who reject His love and rule (2 Peter 2:4–9).

In the here and now, however, we face iniquities. For His all–wise reasons, God has chosen to delay His perfect justice. The psalm writer Asaph struggled with this apparent unfairness of life. He wrote about the wicked who were getting away with their evil deeds, even prospering, while many of the righteous were having troubles (Psalm 73). Concerning the prosperity of the wicked he said, "When I thought how to understand this, it was too painful for me—until I went into the sanctuary of God; then I understood their end" (vv.16,17). By thinking of the sovereign Lord of the universe, Asaph was able to get things back into perspective.

When we struggle with the reality that wicked people are literally "getting away with murder" and all sorts of immorality, we need to remember that "the Lord is…longsuffering toward us, not willing that any should perish but that all should come to repentance" (2 Peter 3:9). The first part of the answer, then, to the problem of suffering is that God uses it to alert us to serious problems. Pain sounds the alarm that indicates something is wrong with the world, with humanity at large, and with you and me. But as we will see in the next section, God not only signals the problems, He also uses troubles to encourage us to find the solutions—in Him.

Why Would God Allow Suffering?—To Direct Us

When a person turns away from God, suffering often gets the blame. But strangely, suffering also gets the credit when people describe what redirected their lives, helped them to see life more clearly, and caused their relationship with God to grow closer. How can similar circumstances have such radically different effects on people? The reasons lie deep within the people, not the events.

A well-known and outspoken media leader publicly denounced Christianity as "a religion for losers." But he has not always felt that way. As a young man he had Bible training, including a Christian prep school. When joking about the heavy indoctrination he received, he said, "I think I was saved seven or eight times." But then a painful experience changed his outlook on life and God. His younger sister became very ill. He prayed for her healing, but after five years of suffering she died. He became disillusioned with a God who would allow that to happen. He said, "I began to lose my faith, and the more I lost it the better I felt."

What makes the difference between someone like him and a person like Joni Eareckson Tada? In *Where Is God When It Hurts?* Philip Yancey describes the gradual transformation that took place in Joni's attitude in the years after she was paralyzed in a diving accident." At first, Joni found it impossible to reconcile her condition with her belief in a loving God. The turning to God was very gradual. A melting in her attitude from bitterness to trust dragged out over three years of tears and violent questioning" (pp.133,134).

A turning point came the evening that a close friend, Cindy, told her, "Joni, you aren't the only one. Jesus knows how you feel—why, He was paralyzed too." Cindy described how Jesus was fastened to the cross, paralyzed by the nails. Yancey then observed, "The thought intrigued Joni and, for a moment, took her mind off her own pain. It had never occurred to her that God might have felt the same piercing sensations that now racked her body. The realization was profoundly comforting" (p.134).

Instead of continuing to search for why the devastating accident occurred, Joni has been forced to depend more heavily on the Lord and to look at life from a long–range perspective. Yancey further says about Joni, "She wrestled with God, yes, but she did not turn away from Him....Joni now calls her accident a 'glorious intruder,' and claims it was the best thing that ever happened to her. God used it to get her attention and direct her thoughts toward Him" (pp.137,138).

This principle that suffering can produce healthy dependence on God is taught by the apostle Paul in one of his letters to the church in Corinth. He wrote: "For we do not want you to be ignorant, brethren, of our trouble which came to us in Asia: that we were burdened beyond measure, above strength, so that we despaired even of life. Yes, we had the sentence of death in ourselves, that we should not trust in ourselves but in God who raises the dead" (2 Corinthians 1:8, 9).

A similar idea can be found in Paul's comments about his physical troubles. The Lord told Paul, "My grace is sufficient for you, for My strength is made perfect in weakness" (2 Cor. 12:9). Then Paul added, "Therefore I take pleasure in infirmities, in reproaches, in needs, in persecutions, in distresses, for Christ's sake. For when I am weak, then I am strong" (v.10).

Suffering has a way of showing how weak our own resources really are. It forces us to rethink priorities, values, goals, dreams, pleasures, the source of real strength, and our relationships with people and with God. It has a way of directing our attention to spiritual realities—if we don't turn from God instead. Suffering forces us to evaluate the direction of our lives. We can choose to despair by focussing on our present problems, or we can choose to hope by recognizing God's long–range plan for us (Romans 5:5; 8:18,28; Hebrews 11).

Of all the passages in the Bible, Hebrews 11 most reassures me that whether life is grand or grotesque, my response needs to be one of faith in the wisdom, power, and control of God. No matter what, I have good reason to trust Him—just as the great men and women of old hoped in Him.

For example, Hebrews 11 reminds us about Noah, a man who spent 120 years waiting for God to fulfill His promise of a devastating flood (Genesis 6:3). Abraham waited many agonizing years before the child whom God had promised was finally born. Joseph was sold into slavery and wrongfully imprisoned, but he finally saw how God used all the apparent evil in his life for a good purpose (Genesis 50:20). Moses waited until he was 80 years old before God used him to help deliver the Jews from Egypt. And even then, leading those faith–deficient people was a struggle (see Exodus).

Hebrews 11 lists people like Gideon, Samson, David, and Samuel, who saw great victories as they lived for the Lord. But in the middle of verse 35 the mood changes. Suddenly we are face–to–face with people who had to endure incredible suffer-ing—people who died without seeing why God allowed them to undergo such tragedies. These individuals were tortured, jeered, flogged, stoned, cut in half, stabbed, mistreated, and forced to live as outcasts (vv.35–38). God had planned that only in the long–range view of eternity would their faithfulness dur-ing hardship be rewarded (vv.39,40).

Pain forces us to look beyond our immediate circumstances. Suffering drives us to ask the big questions of "Why am I here?" and "What's the purpose of my life?" By pursuing those questions and finding the answers in the God of the Bible, we will find the stability we need to endure even the worst that life can inflict because we know that this present life is not all there is. If we know that a sovereign God is standing over all of human history and weaving it all together in a beautiful tapestry that will ulti-mately glorify Him, then we can see things in better perspective.

In Romans 8:18 the apostle Paul wrote, "For I consider that the sufferings of this present time are not worthy to be com-pared with the glory which shall be revealed in us." Paul was not making light of our troubles, but he was telling believers to see our present troubles in light of all eternity. Our problems may indeed be heavy, even crushing. But Paul says that when compared to the incredible glories that await those who love God, even the darkest and most burdensome circumstances of life will fade by comparison.

We need to take time to look at one more example, perhaps the most significant illustration we could consider. The day that Christ hung on the cross is now referred to as Good Friday. At the time, it was anything but a good day. It was a day of intense suffering, anguish, darkness, and gloom. It was a day when Jesus felt all alone. It was a day when God seemed absent and silent, when evil seemed to triumph, and hopes were dashed. But then came Sunday. Jesus rose from the grave. That awesome event put Friday in a different light. The resurrection gave a whole new meaning to what happened on the cross. Instead of being a time of defeat, it became a day of triumph.

We too can look ahead. We can endure our dark "Fridays" and be able to look on them as "good" because we serve the God of Sunday. So when troubles strike, and they will, remember this: God uses such situations to direct us to Him and to the long-range view of life. He calls for us to trust, to hope, to wait.

Why Would a Good God Allow Suffering?— To Shape Us

Athletic coaches like to use the phrase "No pain, no gain." As a high school track star (Okay, maybe I wasn't that great, but I tried hard!), I heard coaches remind us again and again that the tough practice sessions would pay off when we began to com-pete. They were right. Oh, we didn't always win, but our hard work did produce obvious benefits.

I learned a lot about myself during those years. And now I'm learning even more as I discipline myself to jog daily. Many days I would just as soon forget it. I don't want to have to feel the pain of stretching exercises. I would rather not push my body's "radiator system" to the extreme. I would just as soon not have to battle fatigue as I go up the hills. So why do I do it? The gain is worth the pain. My blood pressure and pulse rate are kept low, my middle isn't expanding, and I feel more alert and healthy.

Exercise may have obvious benefits, but what about pain that we don't choose? What about illness, disease, accidents, and emotional agony? What kind of gain can come from those? Is the gain really worth the pain? Let's consider what a fellow–sufferer had to say in Romans 5:3,4. The apostle Paul wrote, "…we also glory in tribulations, knowing that tribulation produces perseverance; and perseverance, character; and character, hope."

Paul introduced his statement about the benefits of suffering by saying "we glory in tribulations." How could he say that we should rejoice or be happy that we are having to endure some painful tragedy? He certainly was not telling us to celebrate our troubles; rather, he was telling us to rejoice about what God can and will do for us and for His glory through our trials. Paul's statement encourages us to celebrate the end product, not the painful process itself. He did not mean we are to get some sort of morbid joy out of death, cancer, deformity, financial reversals, a broken relationship, or a tragic accident.

All these things are awful—a dark reminder that we live in a world that has been corrupted by the curse of sin's effects.

The apostle James also wrote about how we should rejoice in the end result of our troubles. He said, "My brethren, count it all joy when you fall into various trials, knowing that the testing of your faith produces patience. But let patience have its perfect work, that you may be perfect and complete, lacking nothing" (1:2–4).

As we combine the truths of these two passages, we can see how the good and praiseworthy products of suffering are patient perseverance, maturity of character, and hope. God can use the hardships of life to shape us to be more mature in the faith, more godly, more Christ–like. When we trust Christ as our Savior, the Lord does not suddenly zap us so that we become perfect people. What He does is remove sin's penalty and set us on the road that leads to heaven. Life then becomes a time of character development as we learn more about God and how we are to please Him. Suffering has a way of dramatically forcing us to deal with the deeper issues of life. By doing so, we grow stronger and gain maturity.

My grandfather, Dr. M. R. De Haan, spoke about the shaping process of our lives in his book Broken Things. He wrote: " The greatest sermons I have ever heard were not preached from pulpits but from sickbeds. The greatest, deepest truths of God's Word have often been revealed not by those who preached as a result of their seminary preparation and education, but by those humble souls who have gone through the seminary of affliction and have learned experientially the deep things of the ways of God.

The most cheerful people I have met, with few exceptions, have been those who had the least sunshine and the most pain and suffering in their lives. The most grateful people I have met were not those who travelled a pathway of roses all their lives through, but those who were confined, because of circumstances, to their homes, often to their beds, and had learned to depend upon God as only such Christians know how to do. The gripers are usually, I have observed, those who enjoy excellent health. The complainers are those who have the least to complain about, and those dear saints of God who have refreshed my heart again and again as they preached from sickbed–pulpits have been the men and women who have been the most cheerful and the most grateful for the blessings of almighty God (pp.43,44)."

How have you responded to the difficulties of life? Have you become bitter or better? Have you grown in your faith or turned away from God? Have you become more Christ–like in your character? Have you let it shape you and conform you to the image of God's Son?

How do all things work together for good? Perhaps the most quoted part of the Bible during a time of pain and suffering is Romans 8:28. It reads, "And we know that all things work together for good to those who love God, to those who are the called according to His purpose." This verse has often been misunderstood and perhaps misused, but its truth can bring a great deal of comfort.

The context of Romans 8 emphasizes what God is doing for us. The indwelling Holy Spirit gives us spiritual life (v.9), reassures us that we are children of God (v.16), and helps us with our prayers during our times of weakness (vv.26,27). Romans 8 also puts our sufferings in the bigger picture of what God is doing—that God is working out His plan of redemption (vv.18–26). Verses 28 through 39 reassure us of God's love for us, that no one or no thing could ever keep God from accomplishing what He wants to do, and that nothing could ever separate us from His love.

Properly viewed in the context of Romans 8, then, verse 28 powerfully reassures us that God is working on behalf of all who have trusted His Son as Saviour. The verse does not promise that we will understand all the events of life or that after a time of testing we will be blessed with good things in this life. But it does reassure us that God is working out His good plan through our lives. He is shaping us and our circumstances to bring glory to Himself.

Author Ron Lee Davis writes in his book Becoming a Whole Person in a Broken World, "The good news is not that God will make our circumstances come out the way we like, but that God can weave even our disappointments and disasters into His eternal plan. The evil that happens to us can be transformed into God's good. Romans 8:28 is God's guarantee that if we love God, our lives can be used to achieve His purposes and further His kingdom" (p.122).

"But," you may ask, "how can God be in control when life seems so out of control? How can He be working things together for His glory and our ultimate good?" In his book *Why Us?* Warren Wiersbe states that God "proves His sovereignty, not by intervening constantly and preventing these events, but by ruling and overruling them so that even tragedies end up accomplishing His ultimate purposes" (p.136).

As the sovereign Lord of the universe, God is using all of life to develop our maturity and Christ–likeness, and to further His eternal plan. In order to accomplish those purposes, however, God wants to use us to help others, and He wants other people to help us. That's what the next section is all about.

Why Would a Good God Allow Suffering?— To Unite Us

Pain and suffering seem to have a special ability to show us how much we need each other. Our struggles remind us how fragile we really are. Even the weakness of others can bolster us when our own strength is sapped.

This truth becomes very real to me each time I meet with a small group of church friends for prayer and fellowship. During those regular times together, we have shared one another's burdens for a sick child, the loss of a job, workplace tensions, a rebellious child, a miscarriage, hostility among family members, depression, everyday stresses, an unsaved family member, tough decisions, neighbourhood crime, battles with sin, and much more. Many times at the end of those meetings I have praised the Lord for the encouragement that we have given to one another. We have been drawn closer and we have been strengthened as we have faced the struggles of life together.

These kinds of personal experiences in light of Scripture remind me of two key truths:

1. Suffering helps us to see our need of other believers.
2. Suffering helps us to meet the needs of others as we allow Christ to work through us.

Let's take a look at each of these ways God uses pain and suffering for the purpose of uniting us with other believers in Christ.

1. Suffering Helps Us to See Our Need of Other Believers

In describing the unity of all believers in Christ, the apostle Paul used the analogy of a human body (1 Corinthians 12). He said that we need each other to function properly. Paul described the situation this way: "And if one member suffers, all the members suffer with it; or if one member is honoured, all the members rejoice with it. Now you are the body of Christ, and members individually" (vv.26, 27).

In his letter to the Ephesians, Paul spoke of Christ, "From whom the whole body, joined and knit together by what every joint supplies, according to the effective working by which every part does its share, causes growth of the body for the edifying of itself in love" (Ephesians 4:16).

When we begin to recognize all that other believers have to offer us, then we will realize how much can be gained by reaching out to them when we are going through a time of struggle. When troubles seem to knock out our strength, we can lean on other believers to help us find new strength in the Lord's power.

2. Suffering Helps Us to Meet the Needs of Others as we Allow Christ to Live Through Us

In 2 Corinthians 1, the apostle Paul wrote, "Blessed be the God and Father of our Lord Jesus Christ, the Father of mercies and God of all comfort, who comforts us in all our tribulation, that we may be able to comfort those who are in any trouble, with the comfort with which we ourselves are comforted by God" (vv.3,4).

As we saw in the previous section, we need each other because we have something valuable to offer each other. We have spiritual insights and wisdom that we have learned as we have undergone trials of all sorts. We know the value of the personal presence of a loving person. When we experience the comfort of God during a troubling situation, we then have an ability to identify with those people who undergo similar situations.

While preparing to write this booklet, I read about the experiences of people who have suffered greatly, and I spoke with others who were familiar with pain. I searched to find out who helped them most in their time of trouble. The answer again and again has been this: another person who had undergone a similar experience. That person can empathize more fully, and his or her comments reflect understanding that comes by experience. To someone who is burdened down, it often sounds shallow and patronizing to hear another say, "I understand what you are going through," unless that person has gone through a similar situation.

Even though the best comforters are those who have undergone similar situations and have grown spiritually stronger through them, that does not mean that the rest of us are off the hook. All of us have a responsibility to do all we can to empathize, to try to understand, to try to comfort. Galatians 6: 2 tells us, "Bear one another's burdens, and so fulfill the law of Christ." And Romans 12:15 states, "Rejoice with those who rejoice, and weep with those who weep."

Dr. Paul Brand, an expert on the disease of leprosy, wrote, "When suffering strikes, those of us standing close by are flattened by the shock. We fight back the lumps in our throats, march resolutely to the hospital for visits, mumble a few cheerful words, perhaps look up articles on what to say to the grieving.

"But when I ask patients and their families, 'Who helped you in your suffering?' I hear a strange, imprecise answer. The person described rarely has smooth answers and a winsome, effervescent personality. It is someone quiet, understanding, who listens more than talks, who does not judge or even offer much advice. A sense of presence. Someone there when I needed him. A hand to hold, an understanding, bewildered hug. A shared lump in the throat." [69]

It's clear: God made us to be dependent on one another. We have much to offer those in pain, and others have much to offer us as we endure troubles. As we develop that unity, we will experience greater comfort when we recognize that God uses suffering to alert us to the problems of sin, He uses difficulty to direct us to Him, and He can even use problems to make us more like Christ.

How Can You Help?

Right now you may be overwhelmed by pain. The thought of trying to help someone else may seem impossible. At some point along the way, though, as you receive God's comfort, you will be ready to give comfort (2 Corinthians 1). In fact, reaching out to help others may be an important part of the process of your own emotional healing.

Or maybe you have read this booklet with the hope that you will be better able to help a hurting friend or loved one. The suggestions in this section are designed for you as well.

Helping others is risky. Our help may not always be welcomed. We may sometimes say the wrong things. But try to help we must. Jesus' parable of the Good Samaritan (Luke 10:25–37) reminds us that we are responsible to help the hurting people we encounter. Here are some suggestions:

- Don't wait for someone else to act first.

- Be physically present with them if possible and touch their hand or give an appropriate hug.

- Focus on their needs and not on your own discomfort with not having adequate answers.

- Allow them to express their feelings. Don't condemn their emotions.

- Learn about their problem.

- Don't pretend that you never struggle.

- Keep your words brief.

- Avoid saying, "You shouldn't feel that way," or, "You know what you should do."

- Assure them of your prayers.

- Pray! Ask God to help you and them.

- Keep in touch.

- Help them dispel false guilt by assuring them that suffering and sin are not the inseparable twins.

- Help them find forgiveness in Christ if they are suffering due to sin, or if they become aware of some sin as they reflect on their lives.

- Encourage them to recall God's faithfulness in times past.

- Focus on Christ's example and help.

- Remind them that God loves us and cares for us and that He is in control.

- Encourage them to take one day at a time.

- Encourage them to reach out for the help they need (friends, family, pastor).

- Help them to realize that coping with troubles takes time.

- Remind them of God's shepherding love (Ps. 23).

- Remind them of God's control over the universe, both the big and small events of life.

- Don't ignore their problem.

- Don't be artificial in trying to "cheer them up." Be genuine. Be the friend you were to them before trouble hit.

- Show them the love you would like other people to show you if you were in their situation.

- Be a good listener.

- Acknowledge how much they hurt.

- Give them time to heal. Don't rush the process.

Better Than Answers

We cry out for complete answers. God offers Himself instead. And that's enough. If we know that we can trust Him, we don't need full explanations. It's enough to know that our pain and suffering are not meaningless. It's enough to know that God still rules the universe and that He really does care about us as individuals.

The greatest evidence of God's concern for us can be found by looking at Jesus Christ. God loved our suffering world so much that He sent His Son to agonize and die for us, to free us from being sentenced to eternal sorrow (John 3:16–18). Because of Jesus, we can avoid the worst of all pain, the pain of separation from God—forever. And because of Christ, we can endure even the worst of tragedies now because of the strength He puts within us and the hope He sets before us.

The first step in coping realistically with the problem of suffering is to recognize its roots in the universal problem of sin. Have you recognized how much Jesus suffered on the Cross for you to free you from the penalty of sin? Put your trust in Him. Receive His free gift of forgiveness. Only in Him will you find a lasting solution to the problem of pain in your life and in the world.

BUT GOD, IT'S SO UNFAIR!

There is just no way of getting around it—bad things do happen to good Christians. There always will be tragedies that just do not make sense to us, that cause incredible pain so that we cry out to God with the why questions: "Why did this happen?" "Why me? "Why now?" and so forth.

Part of the answer is about God giving us free will—He wants everyone to obey the Ten Commandments, for example, but he gives them the choice, and man's choices affect the lives of others. God created us for fellowship with Him and He would prefer children who love Him, also by choice.

The wages of sin is death which makes us vulnerable to disease, accidents, and other people's choices. Then, there are the outcomes related to natural laws, such as gravity—you can't expect not to fall if you jump off the roof of your house, for example. Sometimes we bring suffering upon ourselves through our own behaviour and actions. If you drive too fast, you could be in an accident and so forth.

God loves us as a parent loves a child and He may correct us because of disobedience or rebellion (Hebrews 12:5–11). We may have to experience trials until we respond to trials as we need to: by learning whatever God wants us to (Hebrews 5:8). Suffering may be permitted to teach patience or acceptance or specifically acceptance of God's sovereign will.

Jesus, God's own son, was not exempt from suffering; why should we be? Our pain may be for a higher purpose for which we have to trust God in His wisdom and in His love for us or to become more Christlike (Philippians 3:10). "And not only (so), but we glory in tribulations also: knowing that tribulation worketh patience and patience, experience; and experience, hope" (Romans 5:4). Often God uses our painful experiences to help minister to someone else later on with our testimony of how God brought us through it. People are often more willing to listen to advice from someone who has "been there" themselves. (2 Corinthians 1:3–4, NIV) says " Praise be to the God and Father of our Lord Jesus Christ, the Father of Compassion, and the God of all comfort, who comforts us in all our troubles, so that we can comfort those in any trouble with the comfort we ourselves have received from God."

There is meaning in suffering, if you are willing to look for it. A tragedy may help us to re–evaluate our priorities. If we manage adversity with grace and with steadfast trust in God, it can be a wonderful testimony for others to encourage them. Even if we never figure out why suffering was allowed in our lives, it is still necessary to choose to accept trials and continue to believe in God's love for us. Is your relationship with God deep enough to enable you to transcend the difficulties and sorrows of this world?

If you have read the chapter on "Meaning in Suffering" and you are still struggling with reconciling your suffering with a loving God, then perhaps you still see your life as "unfair." Some blame their race, nationality, physical traits, social status, economic status, age, or anything else they believe has resulted in what they perceive as greater challenges than others have. Job wished he had never been born because after living a righteous life, he lost everything. Elijah believed he was the only righteous man; Jonah thought it was unfair that he would be required to preach to the pagans of Nineveh and then he felt indignant when the people of Nineveh repented. David resented the fact that the unrighteous prospered.

What about Jesus? Were His circumstances fair? The son of God was born in a barn and rejected by people He knew. He was falsely accused and beaten and tortured and killed for a crime he did not commit. He even felt rejected by His Father on the Cross—for our sakes.

Jesus didn't see Himself as a victim, however; He trusted in God's love for Him in spite of His horrific circumstances. When we feel like victims, we flood ourselves with negative emotions, starting with anger and resentment. When you take the position that your circumstances are unfair, you are really saying that God is unfair and that He is mistreating you or allowing you to be mistreated. Then you can convince yourself that He doesn't really care about you and then you may stop trying to please Him. This only makes things worse, of course, because your resentment toward God affects your fellowship with Him, and in a sense, He can't help you a whole lot until you allow an attitude adjustment.

The truth is that we all deserve to go to hell, "All have sinned and fall short of the glory of God (Romans 3:23) and all of us face unfair circumstances at some point in our lives, "There hath no temptation taken you but such as is common to man" (I Corinthians 10:13). You need to understand that while your circumstances may seem unfair or actually be unfair, God is righteous and just (Romans 3:4).

Elijah did not see the other 7,000 righteous, Jonah did not appreciate God's mercy toward the people of Ninevah, Job did not know that if he kept on trusting God that God would give him back everything he lost twice over. No one, including us, can see the big picture—what God sees. We all, however, have been given God's grace to overcome any temptation, "There hath no temptation taken you but such as is common to man: but God [is] faithful, who will not suffer you to be tempted above that ye are able; but will with the temptation also make a way to escape, that ye may be able to bear it" (1 Corinthians 10:13).

We need to shift our focus from our circumstances to understanding God's nature; He is holy and loving. We are to be led by the Spirit (Galatians 5:16). It is a step of obedience to give thanks for everything, including our past or present situation (1 Thessalonians 5:18). We have to choose to believe Romans 8:28 that "all things are working together for good" for us. In fact, take a minute to brainstorm and make a list of all the benefits that you think God might be able to bring out of your present situation.

Renewing your mind (Romans 12:2) is important here because people get caught up in believing "shoulds" and "oughts." They have their own preconceived ideas about what they should expect from God, what they should expect in their lives, whether these are scriptural beliefs or not. Change your thinking so that you don't demand personal rights anymore. God is in charge. He is Holy. He is just. He is in control of your life and He is acting out of love for you whether you can see that now or not.

We are to continue praising God for who He is, not for what we see or don't see happening in our individual lives. "Put on the garment of praise for the spirit of heaviness" (Isaiah 61:3) It could be that one of the reasons you have been allowed to suffer is so that you will truly come to know God better, that He is loving and kind and merciful. That He is just and good and He can be trusted. He wants us to have child–like faith and what better way to develop that kind of faith then when we have lost everything and need to wholly depend on Him? He wants you to be closer to Him and you can let your circum-stances drive you away from Him or draw you closer to Him.

> Consider it pure joy my brothers, whenever you face trials of many kinds, because you know that the testing of your faith develops perseverance. Beloved, do not think it strange concerning the fiery trial which is to try you, as though some strange thing has happened to you, but rejoice to the extent that you partake of Christ's sufferings, that when His glory is revealed, you may also be glad with exceeding joy.
>
> 1 Peter 4:12–13

Resources:

http://www.wholeperson–counseling.org

WHEN ALL ELSE FAILS

Abraham Lincoln failed the law examination seven times before he finally passed. Charles Carlson developed the process of photocopying in 1938, but had to persevere for twenty–one years before the first Xerox copier was finally manufactured. These two men persevered until they achieved their apparently unattainable goals. I know a woman who faithfully prayed for her husband's salvation; it took over thirty years but that man gave His life to the Lord recently! What's the message here? Never give up!

What about Joseph in the Bible? (Genesis 37–50). He was sold into slavery by his brothers and imprisoned and waited many years to see the fruition of the vision God had given him. Surely, during the many years of mistreatment and betrayal, Joseph wondered where God was and why his life did not make any sense. In spite of his circumstances, in Genesis 39:21 we read, "But the Lord was with Joseph."

Perhaps you are going through a really difficult time. Maybe you have struggled through many tribulations for a number of years as a Christian or had to deal with painful tragedies in your life. Just as God was watching over Joseph and aware of his circumstances the whole time, so God is still with you, watching over you, working everything together for good in your life as He promises (Romans 8:28).

Choices in the Midst of Adversity

Bad things do happen to good Christians. We can expect troubles; they are a certainty. So the first choice (conscious decision) we need to make is to accept the fact that we will have tribulations. "Do not be surprised at the painful things you are now suffering. These things are testing your faith" (1 Peter 4:12–13, ICB).

And why would any of us be exempt from trials anyway? We sometimes believe the lie that if we try to be obedient and serve God in any way we can, then we should be spared from tribulation or pain. Jesus Himself was not spared from suffering or loneliness or temptation to be discouraged. He was misunderstood, unjustly criticized, abandoned in his most difficult hours. Jesus cried out, "My God, My God, why have you forsaken me?"(Matthew 27:46). We know that Jesus had been obedient and we also know that God had not forsaken His own son. Neither has He abandoned you.

The apostle Paul wrote, "In everything we do we try to show that we are true ministers of God. We patiently endure troubles and hardships and calamities of every kind. We have been beaten, been put in jail, faced angry mobs, worked to exhaustion, endured sleepless nights, and gone without food" (2 Corinthians 6:4–5, NLT).

Have we suffered these kinds of trials because of our faith in Jesus Christ? Probably not. Paul was despised, abused, poor and so forth. He could have resigned himself to anger and despair but instead he chose joy.

My brothers, consider yourselves fortunate when all kinds of trials come your way for you know that when your faith succeeds in facing such trials, the result is the ability to endure. Make sure that your endurance carries you all the way without failing, so that you may be perfect and complete, lacking nothing.

James 1:2–4

Imagine the grief God went through when Jesus was crucified. What if, as a parent watching His child suffer in agony, God had decided that He wanted to relieve Jesus' suffering by taking Him down off the Cross and healing Him before His plan for our salvation was carried out?

The most difficult times in our lives result in eternal good somehow. God is a lot more concerned with our character and His higher purposes. "For as the heavens are higher than the earth, so are my ways higher than your ways and my thoughts than your thoughts" (Isaiah 55:9).

Suffering may be what is necessary to draw you closer to Him. Our goal should not be to understand God's motives, but to understand His character and to trust in His promises. Our second decision—because it *is* a *choice*—is to believe that He is a good and loving God who allows suffering for a good and loving reason. If you have given your life to God, then everything that happens to you is uniquely ordained or allowed by God.

Have you received the email forward about the donkey that fell in the well? Someone started shovelling dirt on him there in the well! But the donkey would shake off the dirt and step up a little each time. Eventually, the donkey was able to step out of the well. The moral of the story is that life is going to shovel all kinds of dirt on you. You can allow yourself to be buried by it or you can choose to "shake it off" and come up higher. Never give up!

If we truly want to become more like Jesus then God must take us through trials similar to what Jesus Himself experienced. We cannot be used to help others effectively if we ourselves are despairing as well. Trials equip us to serve others. Paul writes in 2 Corinthians 1:4, "He helps in all our troubles, so that we are able to help others who have all kinds of troubles, using the same help that we ourselves have received from God." It reminds me of the anonymous quote "To have suffered much is like knowing many languages: it gives the sufferer access to many more people."

Can we say like Job, "though he slay me yet will I trust in Him"? (Job 13:15). You've heard the expression "think outside of the box." Well, sometimes we need to "look beyond the suffering."

Learn to view everything, the good and the bad, as a worthwhile experience. Every crisis that you face is a growth opportunity for you to learn to trust God even more than before. Every crisis in your life is also an opportunity for God to manifest His purpose and His power. When you feel that you have lost everything, then you find out that God is everything you need.

Our third choice is to refuse to be discouraged. Jeremy Taylor[70] said "It is impossible for that man to despair who remembers that his Helper is omnipotent." There is every reason to hope for those who are in Christ! We can rely on God for strength for the storms. The very purpose of some of those storms may be to teach us just that—He is faithful and will see us through every adversity. Never give up!

Here is the key, "Whenever trouble comes your way, let it be an opportunity for joy. For when your faith is tested, your endurance has a chance to grow" (James 1:2–3, NLT). True joy is knowing deep down that God is in control and that He can be trusted. The highest joy, however, may come out of the greatest pain, as it motivates us to seek God more than we ever have before.

Conversely, if we stiffen our backs and rail against God's perceived "mistreatment" of us, we will most likely prolong the trial we are experiencing. Be careful that you don't resent God for allowing suffering in your life. It will impede your fellowship with Him and you won't be able to heal and move forward. Better to pray that you will be able to learn whatever He wants you to from whatever you are going through as quickly as possible.

Joel Freeman[71] said that "the highest life toward God may be when you choose to continue loving and praising Him when He allows nothing but suffering in your life." Human logic will fail to explain life's tragedies; faith is about choosing to be obedient in spite of life's tragedies.

The fourth decision to help us accept pain and suffering is the decision to surrender our wills to His rightful sovereignty. Is it your prayer that you live for His honour and glory? Can you tell Him that whatever He allows in your life is okay because you trust Him to work out His higher purposes because you know that He has your best interests at heart?

Let's review our choices in the midst of adversity:

1. We can choose to accept the fact that trials will come our way instead of thinking that we are somehow entitled to be spared from pain in our lives.

2. We can choose to believe that He is a good and loving God who has allowed suffering in our lives for a good and loving reason. We choose to trust in His character, not in what makes sense to us.

3. We choose not to be defeated by our circumstances but to trust in His promises.

4. We choose to yield to His sovereignty and accept His will.

5. We choose to continue to thank God, love Him, serve Him, and praise Him for who He is.

(It may be necessary to "renew" your mind with the word of God: refer to the chapter "It's All About Attitude.")

I think we would all have to agree with Ian MacPherson who said, "The bitterest cup with Christ is better than the sweetest cup without Him."

In his book *Prison to Praise*, Chaplain Merlin Carothers challenges people to actually thank God for their worst circumstances, regardless of how senseless or how painful or how unjust their circumstances may be, no matter how long they have been in pain or how many tragedies they have endured. This kind of prayer is not so much about thanking God for the actual circumstances, rather it is being thankful that:

- You can trust Him to bring good out of it.
- You can trust in His higher purposes.
- You can trust in His sovereign will.
- You can trust in His loving character.
- You can trust in His love for you personally.
- You can trust Him for the strength and grace to endure it.
- He will help you to accept His will if you yield your will to Him.

There is a wonderful story "The Rock" by Carmine Santorelli about God telling a man to move a large rock in front of his cabin. The man laboured from dawn to dusk each day for many days then years trying to move the rock. When he became discouraged, the devil told him that it was an impossible task and that he was a failure. When the man asked God why he was failing, the Lord explained that He had never expected the man to be able to move the rock, only to push on it.

As a result, he was in excellent physical condition and he had fulfilled his real task, which was to be obedient and to trust in God's wisdom. Then God told him He would remove the rock. The moral of the story is that God requires simple, child–like faith in Him. Exercise your faith but remember that it is still God who moves mountains. Never give up!

Whatever your need is today, God is there for you. He never withdraws from you, but you may withdraw from Him or push Him away. God has a plan and a purpose for your life (Jeremiah 29:11). Jesus is your future and your victory, your strength and your peace. Ask God to forgive you today for any wrong attitudes you have had toward Him and/or others. Surrender your heart and your life anew to Him, giving Him everything you have, including your broken heart, your pain, your disappointments, and your discouragement. Never give up!

Seek out pastoral help or consult with a Christian counsellor if you are struggling with ongoing despair. My chapter on resources lists ministries that will pray with you or for you.

"The Lord is near to those who are discouraged, he saves those who have lost all hope"(Psalm 34:18). His love for you is indescribable and beyond human concepts. God says to you *"I will never leave you; I will never abandon you."* Let us be bold, then, and say, "The Lord is my helper, I will not be afraid" (Hebrews 13:5). *Never give up!*

Scriptural Encouragement:

I waited patiently for the Lord's help: then he listened to me and heard my cry. He pulled me out of a dangerous pit, out of the deadly quicksand. He set me safely on a rock and made me secure. He taught me to sing a new song, a song of praise to our God.

Psalm 40:1–3

But Christ as a Son over His own house, whose house we are if we hold fast the confidence and the rejoicing of the hope firm to the end.

Hebrews 3:6

Let us hold fast the confession of our hope without wavering, for He who promised is faithful.

Hebrews 10:23

This hope we have as an anchor of the soul, both sure and steadfast…

Hebrews 6:19

Resources:

Embracing Brokenness: How God Refines Us Through Life's Disappointments by Alan Nelson

FURTHER RESOURCES IN
ALPHABETICAL ORDER

Counseling for Urgent Needs

1–800–suicide

www.samaritans.org

www.newhopenow.org for real time chat

Christian Counseling Books

Therapy—Neil T. Anderson, Terry Zuehlke, Julianne Zuehlke

Psychology, Theology, and Spirituality in Christian Counselling—Mark R. McMinn

The Common Made Holy—Neil T. Anderson

Journal of Psychology and Christianity

Chronic Pain

www.painfoundation.org

Cognitive–Behavioural Therapy (renewing the mind)

Re–training cognitive processes with biblical truths in order to be set free from strongholds of the world, the flesh, and the devil.

Victory Over Darkenss—Neil T. Anderson

Telling Yourself the Truth—William Backus and Marie Chapian

Feeling Good: The New Mood Therapy—David Burns

Taking Every Thought Captive: Spiritual Workouts to Renew Your Mind in God's Truth—Alaine Pakkula

The Lies We Believe—Chris Thurman

The Truths We Must Believe—Chris Thurman

Crossroads Communications

http://www.crossroads.ca/resource/resource.htm A Christian website with over 30 pages of help on any number of topics: senior care, fetal alcohol syndrome, weight loss care, help for incarcerated Christians...

Disassociative Identity Disorder:
(Multiple Personality Disorder)

info@cornerstonechristian.ca Excellent audio/videotape materials

The Life Model: Living from the Heart Jesus Gave You—James Friesen, James Wilder, Anne Bierling, Rick Koepcke, and Maribeth Poole

Breaking the Demonic Network: What is the Core? Restoring shattered lives—Tom R. Hawkins

(www.shieldoffaith.org:Restoration in Christ Ministry)

Trauma and Recovery—Judith Herman

Advanced Studies in TheoPhostic Ministry—Ed Smith

Dungeons and Dragons

http://www.macgregorministries.org/cult_groups/
dungeons_dragons.html

Free Christian Counseling:

mac112355@aol.com

jewess4jesus@comcast.net Rhonda Gordon

http://www.counsellor-on-the-net.comwww.nlm.jesusanswers.com

http://www.ourchurch.com

http://scarletcleansing.tripod.com/http://dmoz.org/society/religion

www.befrienders.org/mainindex.html (not christian)

http://members.truepath.com/cybercounsel.options.html (request not now–jan.2003–swamped)

www.samaritans.org

www.suicidehotlines.com

http://www.users.bigpond.com/kulander

http://users.senet.com.au/~sluchich/

http://www.CB–Counselling.com

http://www.4counselling.com.au

http://www.psychelp–sos.com.au

http://www.jspencer.com.au/servo2.htm

http://www.heritagecounselling.homestead.com/

http://www.netpsych.net.au/

http://www.suzannebarr.com.au/index2.htm

http://www4.tpgi.com.au/users/bms2

Healing
www.christianhealingmin.org

Book: How to Pray for Healing—Che Ahn

Jehovah Witnesses
www.spotlightministries.org.uk Searching questions to ask Jehovah Witnesses.

Joyce Meyer Ministries
http://www.joycemeyer.org/cgi–bin/hfth.
plx?page=hfth&subpage=hfth&page_ref=Nav&section_id=NA

Over 50 articles on topics such as: loneliness, rejection, stress, overcoming fear, prejudice, victory over depression…

Parenting
Leading Teens to Freedom in Christ—Neil T. Anderson

The Seduction of Our Children—Neil T. Anderson

Spiritual Protection for Your Children—Neil Anderson and Peter and Sue Vander Hook

How to Really Love Your Child—Ross Campbell

Relief for Hurting Parents—Buddy Scott

Praise

Prison to Praise, by Merlin Carothers.

How to find freedom from the prison of circumstances.

Prayer Requests

www.cbn.com Online Prayer Requests

The 700 Club Prayer Counselors are available 24 hours a day at (800) 759-0700.

www.worldprayerteam.org

www.Morning–Star.Com—prayer ministry to women

http://www.joycemeyer.org/pray_req.php?page=ministry&subpage=pray_req&page_ref=TopNav&section_id=NA (Joyce Meyer Ministries) Phone: 1–800–727–9673

https://www.crossroads.ca/prayerreq.shtml—Crossroads Family of Ministries

http://www.harvestcm.org/PrayerRequests.htm Harvest Cathedral Ministries

1–800–947–5433 Life Outreach International

Obsessive Compulsive Disorder (OCD):

Family Member Support http://www.nursece.com/onlinecourses/987. html

Online Support Groups

AA—NA, Abuse and Rape, Addictions, ADD, ADHD, Anxiety Disorders, Bipolar, Depression, Caregivers, Depression, Divorce, Eating Disorders, ECT, OCD, Overeaters, PTSD, Relationships, Schizophrenia, Self Esteem, Self Harm, Suicide, Youth Chat:

To sign up for any of the above groups simply e–mail: director@thera-chat.org, and specify what groups you are interested in.

http://www.griefsupportservices.org/newgrief/griefsupportservices/onlinesupportgroup.php has grief support groups, depression, eating disorders and more.

Poetry
http://www.onwingsoffaith.com/garden_treasures.htm Many uplifting Christian poems to encourage you.

Pornography
www.contentwatch.com—computer porn filter program

www.purelifeministries.com—overcoming addiction to pornography.

www.settingcaptivesfree.com

Radio Bible Class
www.rbc.org—has many excellent booklets on:, knowing God, marriage & family, church, the Bible, counselling booklets Christian Living…Also offers online courses.

Ritual Abuse
Overcoming SRA—"Reaching for the Light: A Guide for Ritual Abuse Survivors and Their Therapists" by Emilie P. Rose

Teens
www.newhopenow.org—teen section– volunteers will speak with you in real time chat

www.shakenshine.com—counselling by volunteers

Http://www.domini.org/centerweb/adv.html

http://www.christianhangout.net

http://geocities.com/punkrawkBible/gna.html

Temptation

Facing temptation article Lynda Braun,
www.settingcaptivesfree.com

Theophostics (Prayer Counseling)

Effective when emotions in a current situation far exceed the appropriate level of feeling that should exist due to current stimuli. Healing Childhood Memories. Found to be especially effective in the integration of identities in Disassociative Identity Disorder and many counsellors use theophostics in conjunction with Neil Anderson's "Steps to Freedom in Christ."

Beyond Tolerable Recovery—Ed Smith

Advanced Studies in TheoPhostic Ministry—Ed Smith

REFERENCES

American Psychiatric Association (1994) Diagnostic Criteria from DSM–IV. Washington, D.C.: American Psychiatric Association.

Anderson, Neil T, Zuehlike, T.E., Zuehlke, M.S.(2000). Christ–centered Therapy: The practical integration of Theology and Psychology. Rand Rapids, Michigan: Zondervan Publishing House.

Bilich, M., Bonfiglio, S, Carlson, S. (2000) Shared Grace: Therapists and Clergy Working Together. New York : Haworth Pastoral Press.

Burns, D. et al., (2000)."Rumble in Reno: The Psychosocial Perspective on Depression," Psychiatric Times, 17(8). Health news story: Myths of Depression Challenged.

Burns, David (1980, 1999 revised) Feeling Good–the New Mood Therapy. New York, New York: Avon Books.

Carothers, Merlin R. (1970) Prison to Praise. Plainfield, New Jersey: Logos International.

Cloud, H. & Townsend, J.(1992) Boundaries: When to Say Yes, When to Say No: Take Control of Your Life. Grand Rapids, Michigan: Zondervan.

De Angelis, Barbara (1992) Are You the One for Me? New York, New York: Bantam Doubleday Dell Publishing Group Inc.

Ewing, J.A. "Detecting Alcoholism: The CAGE Questionaire." JAMA 252: 1905–1907, 1984.

Freeman, J.(1987) "God Is Not Fair": Coming to Terms with Life's Raw Deals. San Bernardino, California: Here's Life Publishers.

Fathersloveletter.com

Good Will Publishers Inc.(1962) Portrait of Christ for Newlyweds. Gastonia, North Carolina: Good Will Publishers Inc.

Graham, B (1984) Billy Graham Christian Worker's Handbook. Minnneapolis, Mn:Worldwide Publications.

Johnson, S.L. (1997) 123's Therapist's Guide to Clinical Intervention. San Diego, California: Academic Press.

http://www.kadd.org/Self%20Tests.htm—self–assessment quizzes for alcoholism and addiction.

Kochanek, K.D., Murphy, S.L., Anderson, R.N., & Scott, C. (2004) Deaths: Final data for 2002 National Center for Health Statistics; www.cdc.gov/ncns/fastats/suicide.ntn; United States Department of Health and Human Services Centers for Disease Control and Prevention.

Kubler–Ross, E, Kessler, D. (2005) On Grief and Grieving: Finding the Meaning of Grief Through the Five Stages of Loss. New York, New York: Scribner.

Lewis, C.S. (2001) A Grief Observed. Grand Rapids, Michigan: Zondervan.

McDowell, J.& Stewart, D.(1987) Answers to Tough Questions. Vienna, Virginia: Choice Books.

McIntosh, John L.(2002) American Association of Suicidology, 2002 Summary Data; www.suicidology.org, prepared by , PHD, Professor of Psychology, Indiana University South Bend.

W. Meijer, et al. "Association of Risk of Abnormal Bleeding with Degree of Serotonin Reuptake Inhibition by Antidepressants," Archives of Internal Medicine 2004, 164:2367–2370.

Murray, B & Fortinberry. Depression Facts and Stats. www.upliftpro-gram.com.

National Center for PTSD. Facts About PTSD http://www.ncptsd.va.gov/facts/index.html

National Institute for Mental Health The Numbers Count: Mental Illness in America. www.nimh.nih.gov

New York Times article "Antidepressants Lift Clouds, But Lose 'Miracle Drug' Label, June 30, 2002.

Psychiatric Times, October 1999, Health news story: Antidepressants May Increase Risk of Abnormal Bleeding. "Childhood Trauma, CRF Hypersecretion and Depression."

Savard, Liberty (1997) Breaking the Power. Gainesville, Florida: Bridge–Logos Pub.

Strand, P. Exposing Porn: Science, Religion, and the New Addiction. Www.cbn.com April 2004

http://www.sexaddictionhelp.com/test.html—self–assessment for sex addictions.

The Stages of Dealing with Grief. http://fl.essortment.com/stagesgrief_rbdm.htm

U.S. Public Health Services, The Surgeon General's Call To Action to Prevent Suicide, Department of Health and Human Services, © 1999. www.infoline.org/Crisis/risk.asp

VanOyen Witvliet, C, TE Ludwig, and KL Vander Laan. "Granting forgiveness or harboring grudges: implications for emotion, physiology, and health." Psychological Science 12.2 (2001): 117–23.

Vedantam, S. . "FDA Links Antidepressants, Youth Suicide Risk." Washington Post, 23 February, 2004, page A01.

Warren, R. (2002) The Purpose–Driven Life: What on Earth Am I Here For? Grand Rapids, Michigan:Zondervan.

Weeks, Hal, Howtoheal.org

WHO report on mental illness released October 4, 2001. Health news stories: Depression Link to Heart Disease, Hostility, Depression May Boost Heart Disease www.upliftprogram.com

Word Ministries, Inc. (1989) Prayers that Avail Much, Volume 1, Harrison House Inc, Tulsa, Oklahoma, Tulsa, Oklahoma.

Word Ministries, Inc. (1989) Prayers That Avail Much, Volume 2, Harrison House Inc., Tulsa, Oklahoma: Harrison House

ENDNOTES

1. Michael Fackerell has his own personal website at http://www.christian-faith.com/truestories.html.

2. For more info on Ancient Paths Seminars, go to www.familyfoundations.com

3. http://www.christianity.ca/faith/sharing-faith/2003/09.000.html

4. Adapted and used with permission by Hal Weeks–www.howtoheal.org

5. http://www.joniandfriends.org/about/tadabio.shtml)

6. (Used with permission by Hal Weeks– www.howtoheal.org)

7. Strong's # 907 baptize (bap-tide-O); to immerse, submerge; to overwhelm (i.e. fully wet); used only (in the N. T.) of ceremonial ablution, especially (technically) of the ordinance of Christian baptism: KJV – Baptis, baptize, wash. (DIC)

8. Used with permission– 7/30/2005, http://chaldean.org/Articles/detail.asp?iData=29&iCat=53&iChannel=1&nChannel=Articles

9. Used with permission from Dr. Bill Coleman, pastor of Faith Church, Ontario, Canada)

10. Used with permission from J.B.Nicholson

11. Used with permission from Dean Van Druff –www.acts17-11.com

12. VanOyen Witvliet, C. Ludwig, T.E., Vander Laan, K.L. 2001

13. Story in it's entirety – http://www.gbgm-umc.org/highland/Inspirations/throwing_darts.htm

14. Used with permission by Jacqueline Witt –http://www.angelfire. com/mo3/jacquelinesjunque/index46.html

15. Used with permission from Dr. Bill Coleman, Faith Church, Ontario, Canada

16. Topics Only Provided by Pastor Bill Coleman, Ontario, Canada and used with permission

17. Used with permission from Neil T. Anderson

18. Christ–centered Therapy, Anderson N.T., Zuehlke, T.E., Zuehlke, M.S., (2000) Victory Over the Darkness, by Dr. Neil Anderson

19. Carlson, Bonfiglio, Bilich, 2000–used with permission

20. "Boundaries: When to say Yes, When to Say No" by Cloud, H. & Townsend, J, 1992

21. Used with permission from Neil T. Anderson

22. Used with permission from Hal Weeks–www.howtoheal.org

23. by Victor Matthews in Mark BuBeck's book "The Adversary"–used with permission from Moody Press

24. Father's Love Letter used by permission Father Heart Communications Copyright 1999–2006 www.FathersLoveLetter. com The Father's love letter is one of the tracks in Robert Critchley's CD, Beautiful Tapestry, as well.

25. Used with permission – Bilich, M., Bonfiglio, S, Carlson, S. (2000) Shared Grace: Therapists and Clergy Working Together. New York: Haworth Pastoral Press

26. Bilich et al, 2000

27. Used with permission–In Step Two of Neil T. Anderson's Seven Steps to Spiritual Freedom, 2000

28. from Roy Lessin's book "For Mine Eyes Have Seen Thy Salvation–2006 Roy Lessin. Used by permission from DaySpring Cards. www.dayspring.com

29. Used with permission from Leonard Ingram, PhD, The Anger Institute, Chicago, ILL 60608, www.angermgmt.com

30. Used with permission from Leonard Ingram, PhD, The Anger Institute, Chicago, ILL 60608 www.angermgmt.com

31. This list has been crafted by National Coalition for the Protection of Children & Families. For more information on this organization, please visit www.nationalcoalition.org

32. Used with permission – Savard, Liberty (1997) Breaking the Power. Bridge–Logos Pub

33. Used with permission from the book by Bilich, M., Bonfiglio, S, Carlson, S. (2000) Shared Grace: Therapists and Clergy Working Together. New York : Haworth Pastoral Press.

34. Used with permission from the book by Bilich, M., Bonfiglio, S, Carlson, S. (2000) Shared Grace: Therapists and Clergy Working Together. New York : Haworth Pastoral Press.

35. Bilich et al, 2000.

36. Used with permission from the book by Bilich, M., Bonfiglio, S, Carlson, S. (2000) Shared Grace: Therapists and Clergy Working Together. New York : Haworth Pastoral Press.

37. Bilich et al., 2000

38. Used with permission from the book by Bilich, M., Bonfiglio, S, Carlson, S. (2000) Shared Grace: Therapists and Clergy Working Together. New York : Haworth Pastoral Press.

39. Bilich et al, 2000

40. Strand, P. 2004

41. Used with permission from Rory Reid and Dan Gray from their new book "Discussing Pornography Problems with a Spouse", 2006

42. Used with permission from Gamblers Anonymous– http://www. gamblersanonymous.org

43. Used with permission–Savard, Liberty, 1997, Breaking the Power. Bridge–Logos Pub.

44. National Institute for Mental Health The Numbers Count: Mental Illness in America.www.nimh.nih.gov.

45. WHO report on mental illness released October 4, 2001. Health news stories: Depression Link to Heart Disease, Hostility, Depression May; Boost Heart Disease.

46. DSM–IV, (1994) American Psychiatric Association.

47. Childhood Trauma, CRF Hypersecretion and Depression," Psychiatric Times, October 1999.

48. Molecular Psychiatry, August 2005.

49. David Burns et al., "Rumble in Reno: The Psychosocial Perspective on Depression," Psychiatric Times, 2000, 17(8). Health news story: Myths of Depression Challenged

50. New York Times article "Antidepressants Lift Clouds, But Lose 'Miracle Drug' Label", June 30, 2002.

51. S. Vedantam. "FDA Links Antidepressants, Youth Suicide Risk." Washington Post, 23 February, 2004, page A01.

52. W. Meijer, et al. "Association of Risk of Abnormal Bleeding with Degree of Serotonin Reuptake Inhibition)y Antidepressants," Archives of Internal Medicine 2004, 164:2367– 2370.

53. Rebecca Johnson, MD, director of the Center on Aging at the Sinclair School of Nursing, University of Missouri, Columbia. (http://www. arthritis.org/resources/arthritistoday/2003_archives/2003_09_10_ puppy_love.asp)

54. Sandford, John & Paula, Healing the Wounded Spirit, Tulsa, Ok: Victory House Inc.

55. Johnson, S.L. (1997) 123's Therapist's Guide to Clinical Intervention. San Diego, California: Academic Press.

56. Used with permission —Germaine Copeland, Prayers That Avail Much, Volume 1 Tulsa: Harrison House Publishers, copyright 1989, 1997.

57. www.eharmony.com

58. The Complete TM Marriages Workbook 1999, www.completemarriages.com

59. Prayer by Holley Gerth – Courtesy © 2006 DaySpring Cards. www.dayspring.com

60. Used with permission by Peace at Home Family Shelter, Fayetteville, Ar, toll–free 1–877–442–9811

61. Used with permission by Neil T. Anderson

62. Used with permission from step 6 in Steps to Freedom in Christ by Neil T. Anderson

63. 1. Modification in Culture and Psychiatry, 2nd ed. (Baltimore, MD: Johns Hopkins University Press, 1996), 253. Favazza notes that these criteria were developed with the help of Dr. Richard Rosenthal. Karen Conterio, Wendy Lader, and Jennifer K. Bloom, Bodily Harm: The Breakthrough Healing Program for Self–Injurers (New York: Hyperion, 1998), 23–4.

64. Jan Sutton, Healing the Hurt Within: Understand and Relieve the Suffering Behind Self–Destructive Behavior (Oxford: Pathways, 1999)

65. Jane Wegscheider Hyman, Women Living With Self–Injury (Philadelphia: Temple University Press, 1999), 45–46.

66. Kosterlitz, Hans Walter. (2006). Encyclopædia Britannica. Retrieved February 5, 2006, from Encyclopædia Britannica Premium Service. http://www.britannica.com/eb/article?tocId=9113234

67. Used with permission and taken from the book, Breaking the Power, written by Rev. Liberty Savard (Bridge–Logos Pub. 1997). For more information, see www.libertysavard.com

68. Kurt De Haan, *Why Would A Good God Allow Suffering*, Copyright 1999 by RBC Ministries, Grand Rapids, MI 49555. Reprinted by permission. All rights reserved. Further distribution is prohibited without permission from RBC Ministries.

69. Fearfully and Wonderfully Made, pp.203,204

70. 1613–1667

71. Freeman, 1987